Parsley

Herb of the Year™ 2021

International Herb Association

Compiled and edited by Gert Coleman

IHA HERB OF THE YEAR™

Each year the International Herb Association chooses an **Herb of the Year**™ to highlight. The Horticultural Committee evaluates possible choices based on their being outstanding in at least two of the three major categories: culinary, medicinal, and ornamental. Herbal organizations around the world work together with us to educate the public throughout the year.

Herb of the Year™ books are published annually by the

International Herb Association
P.O. Box 5667 Jacksonville, Florida 32247-5667
www.iherb.org

This book is intended as an informational guide. The remedies, approaches, and techniques described herein are meant to supplement, and not to be a substitute for professional medical care or treatment; please consult your health care provider.

The International Herb Association is a professional trade organization providing education, service, and development for members engaged in all aspects of the herbal industry.

ISBN: 978-0-578-82241-9

*Uniting Herb Professionals for Growth
Through Promotion and Education*

The International Herb Association has some of the most dedicated volunteers who keep the organization afloat, giving their time and talents to ensure that IHA continues to share herbal knowledge and connect those in the profession of herbs. We are deeply indebted to the IHA Board of Directors, the IHA Foundation members, and our webmaster. Thanks for all that you do and for caring enough to move us forward!

Acknowledgments

Best known as a garnish, parsley (*Petroselinum crispum*) is an immensely popular yet often underrated herb. For far too long, parsley has been taken for granted by too many people. Celebrating parsley as the 2021 Herb of the Year™ gives us the chance to rediscover what this valuable and versatile herb does for us and to us!

Packed with fascinating articles, photographs, illustrations, poems, and luscious recipes, this one-of-a-kind anthology explores parsley's extensive ornamental, culinary, medicinal, and poetic qualities as well as its roles in language and culture.

On behalf of the IHA Board and Foundation, I would like to thank each and every contributor.

Wholehearted thanks to **Dr. Arthur O. Tucker** and **Chuck Voigt** for the botany and cultivation of this paragon in the herb garden; to **Tina Marie Wilcox** for the scientific reasons why parsley seed can be so persnickety and to **Susan Belsinger** for the folkoric aspects of the same; to **Kathleen Connole** for collating parsley relatives in both family and name as well their many indigenous uses; to **Bevin Cohen** for highlighting the lesser known Hamburg Parsley; and to **Marge Powell** for an in-depth look at one of parsley's most redolent cousins, asafoetida.

Delicious, nutritious parsley serves as a culinary workhorse, playing well with other herbs and flavorings, yet seldom taking center stage. Many thanks to the excellent, talented cooks **Susan Belsinger**, **Kathleen Connole**, **Pat Crocker**, **Karen England**, **Donna Frawley**, **Steven Lee**, **Carol Little**, **Cooper T. Murray**, **Diann Nance**, **Karen O'Brien**, **Holly and Osamu Shimizu**, **Nancy Scarzello**, **Jane Hawley Stevens**, and **Skye Suter** for highlighting parsley's versatility as a congenial complement to sauces, salads, soups, vegetables and meats, grains, and dessert. Their fabulous smorgasbord of recipes, experience, expertise, and dedicated research makes clear why parsley has always been invited to feasts and parties.

Medicinally, the parsley family has many proven values with some poisonous relatives to watch out for. Utilized as medicine centuries before it became a culinary herb, all parts are used in healing. The leaves are strong, roots stronger, and seeds the strongest. Many thanks to **Janice Cox** for easy-to-use natural beauty recipes; to **Davy Dabney** for tracing parsley's medicinal history; for **Daniel Gagnon**'s masterful medical herb profile; to **Carol Little** for practical ways to add parsley to our lives; and to **Jane Hawley Stevens** for helping us to respect parsley as both food and medicine.

For revealing the essential parsley with discerning eyes, many thanks to the talented illustrators **Alicia Mann, Skye Suter**, and **Gail Wood Miller**; and the inspiring photographers who contributed this year: **Susan Belsinger, Peter Coleman, Karen England, Deb Jolly, Pat Kenny, Theresa Mieseler, Cooper T. Murray, Diann Nance, Stephanie Parello, Richter's**, and **Skye Suter**. Special thanks once again to **Susan Belsinger** for her advice, guidance, and expertise in capturing parsley as seeds, leaves, flowers, and roots. She is truly a cheerleader for the Herbs of the Year!

Special thanks to the poets for celebrating parsley in words and images: **Susan Belsinger, B.V. Marshall, Stephanie Parello**, and **Shirley Russak Wachtel**.

Deep gratitude to the valuable second readers for cogent advice, insight, and keen-eyed proofreading: **Susan Belsinger, Kathleen Connole, Karen England, Skye Suter**, and **Chuck Voigt**. Your time and efforts make this a better book.

Warm, heartfelt appreciation to the hard-working board and foundation members who so generously give their time, energy, and expertise to keep IHA moving forward as a viable herbal organization.

It was a pleasure to work once again with **Heather Cohen**, book designer extraordinaire, whose patience and expertise have helped make this an amazing book.

Many thanks to my husband **Peter** for his photos, sense of humor, and appreciation for all things parsley, and to my children **Lorraine** and **Ian** for living the herbal life with me. And to new puppy **Shadow** for some welcome distractions!

Parsley is my fifth and final book as editor. Words cannot express my gratitude to the wonderful folks who have contributed in so many ways. I have learned a great deal and am humbled to be part of such an enthusiastic and extensive herbal family. Parsley symbolizes both gratitude and festivity, a good plant to end with. **Kathleen Connole** will capably take the reins next year with *Viola*.

~Gert Coleman, Editor

Italian flat-leaved parsley seedlings started in seed flat, planted in Promix.
Susan Belsinger

Table of Contents

Healing Parsley

Parcel or leaf celery (*Apium graveolens* var. *secalinum*) in stone pot. *Skye Suter*

Lucifer's Bounty. *Alicia Mann*

Growing
&
Knowing
Parsley

Flat-leaved parsley harvested with blossoms. *Pat Kenny*

Parsley, a Garnish

B.V. Marshall

Look down at your plate and the green sprigs
that defy the jus, the gratins, and the edible alliums.
Just chewing that small verdant spray
reduces all the bad odors from potential kisses and coos.
It covers. It reduces. It does more than it should.

Once, on an island, a general slaughtered his many
thousand captives because they could not roll
the 'R's' in the name of the herb in a strange tongue.
They knew the herb but could not say its foreign name.

It is like the foreign term dropped into a poem.
You will use it as a garnish never glory.
It is the supporting player, never the star of the meal.
There are very few recipes for parsley stew.

Heat will wilt even the stems. So, you believe
it is too delicate to support half a dream.
Yet those histories we must devour
Like that of the general and his slaughters
they end up bitter and raw in our mouths
and our hearts so that we may live.

Whatever nourishes us from the *saignant* meat
and the hairy roots yanked from the wretched soil
is more true than belief because we finish
this meal with the small green sprig.

Parsley with borage as supporting player in Toronto Botanical Garden.
Pat Kenny

Benjamin V. Marshall earned a BA from Kean University and an MFA from University of Massachusetts, Amherst. His plays and workshops include *Boom Box* at HBO's new writers workshop; *Henry's Bridge* at Theatre for a New City; The Red Train Interact Theatre (Philadelphia); *The Balcony Goat* at Luna Stage (NJ); and short play festivals in AK, CT, Montreal, Canada, and Melbourne, Australia. He has published poetry, short fiction, and essays in literary and small presses. A proud member of the Dramatists Guild, and Professor of English at Middlesex County College in NJ, Ben has received fellowships from the Geraldine R. Dodge Foundation, the VCCA, the Helene Wurlitzer Foundation, the National Endowment for the Humanities as well as five playwriting fellowships from the NJ State Council on the Arts. His play *Beasts and Cakes: The Chronicles of Phillis Wheatley* was selected for the first Metzler New Play Festival at AD Players in Houston.

Parsley from *The Culinary Herbal*

Arthur O. Tucker and Susan Belsinger

Petroselinum crispum

Parsley is the first herb that most Americans recognize on sight because it is the most-used herb in the United States, although it may be one of the most misunderstood herbs in the garden. Its most common use is as an uneaten, curly-leaved green garnish, especially on restaurant dinner plates. It is a shame that this garnish is usually thrown away because the leaves are really quite high in vitamins A, B1, B2, and C; niacin, calcium, and iron.

The smell and taste of this vibrant herb is pleasantly green and herbaceous. Elsewhere in the world, parsley plays a key role in a variety of prepared foods; it is used fresh in salads and sauces or added towards the end of cooking to just about any savory dish. Parsley is the main ingredient in *salsa verdes* and can be used as an alternative or supplement to basil pesto, and the root of the Hamburg or turnip-rooted type is consumed. Parsley is a key ingredient to many herbal blends; it combines well with just about any other herb, supporting their flavors—sometimes tempering a strong-flavored herb—or complementing a milder one. The clean, delicate flavor also provides a breath freshener.

Our Picks

The bright green, fernlike leaves provide a delightful accent in the sunny herb garden and make an excellent edging. Three types of parsley are grown in the United States: common (curled-leaf, var. *crispum*); plain (flat-leaved or Italian, var. *neapolitanum* Danert); and Hamburg or turnip-rooted [var. *tuberosum* (Bernh.) Crov.]. The first two are used in sauces, stews, soups, prepared meat products, and condiments, while the latter's large, edible root is considered a vegetable.

Parsley in raised bed with floating row cover hoops. *Susan Belsinger*

Many cooks maintain that the Italian flat-leaved parsley has a more pronounced flavor. In reality, this is due more to texture than chemistry; the curly leaved parsleys are fluffy and airy, dispersing the parsley flavor into a cotton-candy type of delivery vehicle.

Curly-leaved cultivars include many very similar ones, so take your pick: 'Afro', 'Banquet', 'Bravour', 'Curlina', 'Dark Moss Curled', 'Decorator', 'Deep Green', 'Envy', 'Evergreen', 'Ferro', 'Forest Green', 'Improved Market Gardener', 'Moss Curled', 'Paramount', 'Perfection', and 'Sherwood'. Flat-leaf types include 'Perfection', 'Plain', and 'Plain Italian Dark Green'.

In Italy, the cultivar called 'Catalogno', with its long, thick stems and large, dark, flat, green leaves is considered to be the true Italian parsley, while other flat-leaved parsley selections are *commune* (common or ordinary). In the United States, few firms sell this variety, which is usually listed as 'Giant Italian'. It is superior in flavor and yield to other flat-leaved parsleys.

Growing Basics

Biennial to 27 inches
Can withstand frost
Full sun
Moist, not constantly wet
Well-drained garden loam; pH average 6.2

Cultivation and propagation

Seeds (technically fruits known as schizocarps containing two mesocarps) have slow and irregular germination, with 10 and 28 days being allowed for the first and last germination counts, respectively. Parsley's slow and erratic germination has given rise to the fanciful tale that the seed has to go to Hell nine times and back before it will germinate.

The slow germination can be attributed in part to a high concentration of heraclenol in the seeds, a coumarin, which is easily leached out with water. Germination thus can be enhanced by soaking the seeds in aerated water for three days at 77°F, draining, rinsing, and then sowing 1/4-inch deep in a fine seedbed.

Seed started indoors and transplanted into pots shows a more rapid and uniform germination without special treatment, probably because of constant moisture levels and warm soil temperatures. Parsley presents no problems as a transplant as long as it is properly hardened off for increased light and decreased temperature before it is planted in the garden.

In other aspects, parsley should be treated as a leafy green vegetable and grown in rich, moist soil with good drainage and a pH of 5.3 to 7.3.

Harvesting and preserving

Although parsley is a biennial, it occasionally blooms the first year, which reduces yields; parsley that is subjected to thirty days of temperatures below 40°F will flower. Parsley in its second year is usually useless as an herb because the leaves turn bitter after the flower stems rise from the center of the plant in early spring. Thus, when grown for its foliage, parsley is considered as an annual.

Parsley may be harvested by hand continuously throughout the year as a culinary green. The outer leaves should be clipped to 1 to 3 inches above the crown. Up to three sowings of seeds may be possible in some states for harvests April to December, and the home gardener will find that a cold frame will provide fresh parsley all winter. Since dried parsley loses much of its flavor, use parsley fresh from the garden or buy it as it is readily available throughout the year.

Susan Belsinger loves doing research on and growing each new herb of the year. Back in 1995 when IHA first began choosing an herb of the year, all of the common, most beloved, and popular herbs were chosen—except for parsley. It was so common it was passed right by; after all it is a fresh herb that we can find in every supermarket. After much lobbying and 25 years of celebrating the Herb of the Year™, parsley is finally receiving its due. Hoorah!

Over the years, Susan has been honored to work with her mentors. Linda Ligon, herbal visionary, businesswoman, owner and publisher of Interweave Press and *Herb Companion* and *Herbs for Health*, supported the herbalists and herbal community for years and published seven of Susan's books, many of them co-authored with Carolyn Dille. In 1996, Susan co-authored *Basil, An Herb Lover's Guide* with Thomas DeBaggio (Interweave Press) and co-authored *The Culinary Herbal* with Arthur O. Tucker in 2016 and *Grow Your Own Herbs* in 2019 (Timber Press). She sure misses (as we all do) being able to herborize with these herbal legends.

Art Tucker, Emeritus Professor of Botany at Delaware State University, spent more than fifty years using, researching, writing, and teaching about herbs in popular and scientific media. Art served on the IHA board for many years with enthusiasm, humor, and dignity. He inspired countless students and herbalists to grow healthier plants, bring in better harvests, and simply enjoy herbal flavors and fragrances more fully.

Chopping parsley with a mezzaluna on a wooden board is a pleasant kitchen task. *Susan Belsinger*

Flat and curly leaf parsleys growing side-by-side in a clay container.
Susan Belsinger

Parsley as Houseplant

Parsley is the crown of cookery. It once crowned man; it now crowns his food. Irma Goodrich Mazza, *Herbs for the Kitchen*

Even though parsley is readily available in supermarkets all year long, you can grow it as a houseplant. Parsley plants prefer cooler house temperatures, between 60° to 65° F, and a deep container with drainage holes. Water occasionally; like most herbs, it does not like "wet feet". Place in the brightest light possible, preferably near east- or west-facing windows. Snip off parsley leaves as needed, using the older, outer leaves first. Use it generously in soups, salads, herb butters, vinegar, and salts. It makes a delicious addition to green drinks.

Growing Parsley from Seed to Garden—

Overcoming Parley's Devilish Germination Inhibitor and the Problematic Propensity to First Spring Bolt

Tina Marie Wilcox

Parsley is a biennial culinary herb with three major varieties that are native to Europe. They are in the Apiaceae family and so are related to celery, dill, cilantro, and chervil. Curled or common parsley, *Petroselinum crispum* var. *crispum*, is the familiar plate garnish that introduced many Americans to the herb. *P. crispum* var. *neapolitanum*, the flat leaf or Italian parsley, has a stronger flavor. This gardener learned that real chefs prefer this one for cooking after joining the International Herb Association. The Hamburg or turnip-rooted parsley, *P. crispum* var. *tuberosum*, is grown as a root vegetable. The Hamburg is growing in the Heritage Herb Garden for the first time in 2020 because parsley is to be celebrated as the Herb of the Year™ 2021.

At the Ozark Folk Center State Park in Mountain View, Arkansas, the Heritage Herb Garden has planted Italian flat leaf parsley in the Kitchen Garden and sold the plants that we have purchased as plugs or grown from seed in the greenhouse. Three years ago we received a flat of plugs in 3-inch pots that arrived in February and began to bolt in March. We asked for credit on that order because parsley leaves become bitter when the plants flower; it would not be proper to sell them.

Slow germination of parsley seed was never a big problem in our greenhouse. The old adage that parsley has to go nine times to the devil before it germinates was just an expected fact. Seeds of all kinds are planted in 3-inch pots in moist germination medium, then watered in well and covered with a plastic dome. The domes discourage evaporation and fungus gnats until germination. The flats are set on heat mats under grow bulbs. Those seeds that need scarification or a period of cold are given what they need. Every kind of seed just comes up in its own way in its own time—or not.

Last year the garden team planted 'Giant Italian' parsley seed in December in preparation for spring sales and planting. Once again, the parsley bolted as soon as temperatures warmed in late April. This was a conundrum that needed a solution. Biennials are supposed to grow lots of leaves the first year and then bolt to flower the second season.

The greenhouse at the park houses a host of tender garden specimens and sales stock. Space becomes a major issue as spring approaches. After the parsley and other hardy seeds germinate and are transplanted up to 3 1/2-inch pots, they are moved out to an unheated cold frame to harden off. This frees up room inside the greenhouse for the less hardy. In addition, insect, scale and mite pests are not as active in the cold frame.

In researching the problem of early bolting of parsley, I went first to *The Encyclopedia of Herbs: A Comprehensive Reference to Herbs of Flavor and Fragrance* by Thomas DeBaggio and Arthur O. Tucker. They attribute parsley seeds' slow germination to the coumarin *heraclenol*, which is present in the seed coat. Thankfully, heraclenol is water soluble. They recommend soaking the seeds in aerated water for three days at 77°F, draining, rinsing, and immediately sowing. I imagined placing parsley seeds in a small fish bowl with an aquarium bubbler on the heat mat to accomplish this exact soaking method. We have found that soaking the seeds overnight and then rinsing before planting gave satisfactory germination within two weeks.

Heraclenol is a germination inhibitor contained within the seed coat of many Apiaceae species. This is important to know if you grow herbs from seed. Soak and rinse the seeds from this family. Do not use the soaking water to irrigate other seeds. Keep the seeds moist until they germinate. They require darkness to germinate as well, so be sure to plant the seeds 1/4-inch deep in soil or germination medium.

The problem of early bolting was also addressed by DeBaggio and Tucker. Like so many things in life, it's all about timing. In the future, our parsley seed will be sown in early February for April planting and kept inside the warm greenhouse until March. Heed their words: "Parsley that is subjected to thirty days of temperatures below 40°F will flower."

When you purchase pots of parsley, pay attention to important things. How many seedlings are in each pot? Many growers sow many seeds in each pot.

These little plants must be separated when set out in the garden so that each achieves greatness. Second, how rootbound are they? Rapid spring growth is going on inside the pot as well as on top. And did you know that it is considered bad luck to transplant parsley and the growing of parsley is the woman's domain?

Be you brave woman or man gardener, have the watering can at the ready when you plant your potted parsley. Do this work in the early morning, late evening, or on a cloudy day. Create a shallow saucer in the prepared soil, not too deep, then fill it with water until it puddles. Pop the parsley out of the pot and set it in the slurry. Extend the fingers of both hands under the roots and gently tickle the roots outward from the center, freeing the roots from the cylindrical or cube shape they have conformed to while developing inside the pot. Mix the potting medium with the native soil as you liberate the roots so that they are settling outward and down in a mud pie of the familiar and the new. Support the plant while you adjust the level of the crown so that is not too deep or too shallow by adding soil under the roots or removing some. When it is oriented just right, press your palms around the plant and gently press down to be sure all of the roots have contact with soil and air bubbles are forced out. Water again lightly and move on. If there are more than one plant in the pot, keep the ones in waiting wet and out of direct sun. Finally, mulch under the leaves with straw to retain moisture, suppress weeds, and enjoy a cleaner harvest.

Until deer discovered the Kitchen Garden at the Ozark Folk Center, parsley was perpetual. Bolted plants were left to bloom and ripen seed. The seeds remained in place on the plants long after the foliage had browned. They would fall to the earth after the stems could no longer support the umbels. Over winter seedlings would germinate in the beds and paths. These transplanted easily to neat rows. Some seed would remain in the soil until the next winter and so on. For many years there was always first year parsley to cut for the kitchen and second season parsley setting seed. Now parsley is deer candy in the Kitchen Garden and is munched down to the ground before the summer sun can energize the plants into vigorous growth. I will continue to allow parsley to perpetuate naturally at home, safely within a garden protected by chain link and electric fencing.

In the Herb of the Year garden, inside the Craft Village protected by a high fence, nine varieties of parsley are thriving. Women have obtained and shared the seeds, sown them, and waited while they took their own sweet time to germinate, and finally women transplanted the seedlings into the garden. All the superstitions are true as far as I can tell, except for the bad luck parts.

Fresh breath and delicious dishes are ours now and for the foreseeable future, thanks to botanical science and herbal mentors who help us to understand persnickity parsley.

Informative signage in the Herb of the Year bed in the Heritage Herb Garden at the Ozark Folk Center, Mountain View, Arkansas. *Susan Belsinger*

References

Tucker, Arthur and Thomas DeBaggio. *The Encyclopedia of Herbs: A Comprehensive Reference to Herbs of Flavor and Fragrance.* Timber Press, 2009.

Tina Marie Wilcox has been the head gardener and herbalist at the Ozark Folk Center's Heritage Herb Garden in Mountain View, Arkansas, since 1984. She tends the gardens, plans and coordinates annual herbal events, and facilitates the production of sale plants, seeds and herbal products for the park. She is a well-seasoned herbal educator, entertainer and, with Susan Belsinger, co-authored *the creative herbal home*.

Tina currently serves as president of the International Herb Association. She is a member of the Herb Society of America-Ozark Unit and was awarded the Nancy Putnam Excellence in Horticulture Award 2017 by the Herb Society of America. Tina's philosophy is based upon experiencing the joy of the process, perpetrating no harm, and understanding life through play with plants and people. Contact Tina at braidnboots@gmail.com.

In Need of Parsley

Charles E. Voigt

Introduction

Parsley was the first true herb that I ever knew and grew, although that was before I had encountered what the term *herb* really meant, in a culinary sense. For me, it was a fragrance that emerged when the big bag of seeds arrived from the local Future Farmers of America chapter, in the box from a mail order seed company, or as I was memorizing the descriptions on seed packets at the local Sears store. Although many types of seeds have characteristic aromas, it was always parsley that predominated when the seal was broken on the package. This smell always brings back memories of my burst of gardening zeal brought on by the first warming days of spring.

In those innocent days, I would probably have classed parsley as a pretty, leafy green vegetable, one that looked good in the garden and spruced up a 4-H garden display at the county fair. How much of this parsley actually got consumed in our family is probably a very small amount, near to zero. Adding it to dishes would have been considered "fancy" and would rarely, if ever, be done. Using a sprig as a garnish might have brought it into the kitchen and onto my plate, but then it was usually pushed aside while getting to the meat and potatoes. My unaccustomed palate would have been a bit shocked by its intensity.

As it was for me, parsley is the first herb that most Americans recognize on sight, because it is the most-used herb in the U.S. Near the farm garden where I first grew parsley is a huge herb farm, which freeze-dries hundreds of acres of fresh herbs every year. They grow and process both curly and flat leaf parsley, over a hundred acres of each. What a contrast to my little eight-foot row! If you've had freeze-dried parsley or chives anywhere in the world, chances are good that it came from Van Drunen Farms in Momence, Illinois.

How sad it is that I grew such a nutritional powerhouse every year, but just as routinely ignored it in the good old days. While it is widely recognized as a plate garnish and palate cleanser, the benefits of consuming it have eluded modern Americans until fairly recently. It has been said that parsley may be the most nutritious thing on the plate, ounce for ounce. Let me tell you more about this underappreciated garden gem.

History and Lore

The genus name, *Petroselinum*, is derived from the Greek for rock, *petros*, because it was found on cliffs, rocks, and old walls, and *selinum*, celery, which it somewhat resembled. It was dubbed *rock celery*. The specific epithet, *crispum*, refers to the curled leaves of many common cultivars.

The leaf, root, and fruit of parsley have been used for hundreds of years in folk medicine. Pliny considered it to be one of the most important plants for its medicinal value. In ancient Greece, it was used in funeral processions because it was associated with death and oblivion. The legend says that parsley appeared where the blood of Greek hero Archemorus was spilled when he was eaten by serpents. Parsley was strewn over corpses to mask the odor of decaying flesh. It was woven into wreaths for graves or was sometimes planted there to grow into a green carpet. To be "in need of parsley" meant that one was seriously ill, and most likely near death.

Winning athletes were given crowns or wreaths of parsley because Hercules had chosen it for his garlands. Parsley leaves were fed to racehorses to improve their stamina and often worn at Greek banquets to absorb the vapors from the wine and keep men from becoming inebriated. Chewing parsley helps to absorb the odors of strong-smelling foods, such as garlic and onions. Romans also used it to cover up alcohol on the breath and as a digestive aid during extended orgies. Gladiators ate parsley before entering the arena for combat.

The species is thought to be native to Sardinia, Turkey, Algeria, Lebanon, and other Mediterranean/Middle Eastern areas, where it still grows wild, although it has become naturalized in many locations around the world. The Romans introduced it to England, and the English took it with them throughout their extensive empire. It probably arrived in the American colonies in the mid-seventeenth century.

Since parsley is slow to germinate, a superstition arose that it had to travel to Hell and back seven (or nine) times before it could germinate and emerge from the soil. It was also thought that only a witch could grow it well, and, for a good harvest, it should be planted on Good Friday or by a pregnant woman. It was never transplanted for fear of displeasing the herb and bringing bad luck to the one who tried to transplant it. Others believed that only in households presided over by a strong woman could it flourish, reverse misogyny at its most blatant.

Botany

Petroselinum crispum is the species name of cultivated parsley. Three main botanical varieties exist: *Petroselinum crispum* var. *crispum* is the curly leaf type, *Petroselinum crispum* var. *neapolitanum* is the flat leaf or Italian one, and *Petroselinum crispum* var. *tuberosum* is the parsnip-rooted or Hamburg variety. All are biennial herbs in the Apiaceae (formerly Umbelliferae) plant family. In the first year of growth, the plant maintains a rosette form of growth, with all leaves arising from an extremely short stem near ground level. Elongated petioles (not stems) hold the tripinnately-divided leaf blades aloft. Leaflets are curled or crisped in *P.c.* var. *crispum* and flattened in both *neapolitanum* and *tuberosum* varieties.

In the early summer of the second year, the plant bolts a seed stalk up to a yard or more in height. Flowers are borne in umbels, which resemble the ribs of an upside-down umbrella. Individual flowers are greenish-yellow, have five petals and five stamens. These produce tiny fruits which are oval, gray-brown, and ribbed when mature.

Roots are white and of various thicknesses and can be a foot or more in length. In the first season, these are used for carbohydrate storage, which is then utilized in the second season to mature the flower stalk and seeds. The *P. c. tuberosum* variety has been selected with especially large storage roots, which can be eaten like parsnips or carrots.

A second species of this genus, *Petroselinum segetum* (corn parsley), is native to Western Europe, from Great Britain and the Netherlands southward through France to Italy, Spain, and Portugal. It is also edible with a similar flavor to *P. crispum*, although it is not cultivated to any great degree. It can be found growing wild in grasslands, hedgerows, and riverbanks. It is becoming scarcer as agriculture intensifies in its native range. Compared to the common garden parsley, the leaves of this species are narrower, more lanceolate, and only singly pinnate.

Nutritional Value

Parsley is a powerhouse of vitamins and minerals. Vitamin A, B vitamins such as thiamin, riboflavin, and niacin, vitamin C (much more per volume

The umbels of parsley have white to yellowish flowers, each with five petals and five stamens. *Susan Belsinger*

than oranges), calcium, potassium, zinc, iron, and copper are all present. In addition, boron and fluorine in parsley give added strength to bones. It is also a good source of folate. The herb's essential oils contain such compounds as limonene, eugenol, and myristicin, which give the herb its unique aroma as well as anti-fungal, antioxidant, anti-inflammatory, and antiseptic properties. Parsley also contains flavonoids like apigenin and luteolin, which boost the anti-inflammatory and antioxidant benefits of parsley. Because of its richness in all these substances, it has been recommended as being useful in easing the pain of arthritis.

Medicinal Use

Traditionally, parsley fruits were used primarily as a stomachic or carminative (aids digestion or relieves gas), and the root as a diuretic to increase the flow of urine. Parsley seed also has a reputation as an emmenagogue and abortifacient (stimulates menstrual flow and abortion). In addition, it has been given credit for curing a whole range of ailments, such as diabetes, liver and kidney ailments, and venereal disease. There is less evidence of these latter claims. Parsley tea has been prescribed for young female patients with bladder problems. While seeds have some mild stomachic and diuretic action, these effects are fairly mild. On the other hand, distilled parsley volatile oil is toxic undiluted, and under no circumstances should be administered to pregnant women.

A major component of the oil of parsley leaves, myristicin, inhibits tumor formation and increases the detoxifying action of the enzyme system glutathione S-transferase. Some see it as a possible cancer-fighting agent. In addition, furocoumarins from the leaves are antimicrobial. Roots have both diuretic and laxative properties. The German Commission E has approved parsley for use in the prevention and treatment of kidney stones.

In folk tradition, parsley has been used to promote menstruation, facilitate childbirth, and increase female libido. Leaf poultices have been used to alleviate breast tenderness in lactating women. Similar poultices have been used to soothe tired, irritated eyes, and speed the healing of bruises. Juice will relieve the itch and sting of insect bites and may work as a mosquito repellant. Parsley juice has been used to lighten freckles, and inhibits the secretion of histamine, making it useful in treating hives and relieving other allergy symptoms.

Culinary Use

Parsley is a multi-functional herb which can be used as a garnish, with meats, vegetables, soups, and much more. It has a starring role in prepared foods around the world. Parsley pesto can be used as a substitute for, or in combination with, basil pesto. Italian gremolata is a simple blend of parsley, garlic, and lemon zest. Middle Eastern cuisine uses it liberally in tabbouleh and falafel. In the Burgundy region of France, it is used with ham in aspic, with garlic butter and snails, and in *persillade*, a fine mince of garlic and parsley added at the last minute to sautés, grilled meats, and poultry. Belgians and Swiss love fondue with fried parsley leaves on the side. The Japanese deep fry them in tempura batter. Mexicans and Spaniards use it as a major ingredient in salsa verde. The English make parsley jelly.

Parsley is famous for its ability to blend well with other herbs. It can also wake up the flavors in leftovers or carry-out foods. Adding it with butter to a baked potato raises this staple to a new level of flavor. Parsley petioles (often mistakenly called "stems") are a major component of *bouquet garni*, used to infuse flavor into brines, sauces, soups, or stocks. Parsley leaf blades can be added to potato salad, coleslaw, green salads, and grain salads. Parsley can lighten the intensity of garlic or strong-smelling fish in a dish. In a light-colored sauce, the petioles are used rather than the leaf blades to avoid imparting a green color to the sauce.

Both on TV cooking shows and in culinary literature, there is a pretty universal belief that the flat leaf varieties of parsley have more intense flavor than the curled ones. How significant this difference may be is a matter for discussion. Because of the curly nature of the moss curled varieties, they may not play as easily on the tongue as the flat forms. Whichever is available should be adequate, but personal preference can guide purchases. Parsley leaf flavor seems to blend a bright green grassy flavor with hints of citrus, clove, and nutmeg, followed by a mineral aftertaste.

Hamburg parsley root can be used similarly to carrots or parsnips, although parsley roots do not store as long or as well as either once dug and out of the ground. They will store in the ground over winter, if given protection in colder climates. Leaves of the Hamburg parsley can be used the same as flat leaf varieties.

Since the parsley rosettes grow down at soil level, care should be taken to thoroughly wash the leaf blades and petioles before use. The curly varieties, in particular, will benefit from a brief soak in cool water before swishing and rinsing to remove any remaining soil particles. No one likes grit in parsley

Store cut parsley stems in a jar or glass of water. These are the fresh ingredients for the Italian garnish gremolata: parsley, lemon zest and garlic. *Susan Belsinger*

or spinach. Unwashed, parsley will store in the refrigerator for up to a week. After that it begins to yellow and lose its pungency.

Other Uses

In crafts, parsley can be used as a border for tussie mussies, or as a green filler in other small flower arrangements. The flat leaf type works well in pressed flower compositions.

In the landscape, parsley's bright green, fern-like foliage makes it a great accent or edging plant in the garden. Its rosette form of growth keeps it well in bounds without any added maintenance.

In cosmetics, the leaves can be infused in water to make a good hair tonic and conditioner. It can also be added to a body lotion to treat dry skin. An infusion of the leaves is both soothing and cleansing when added to bathwater. Parsley oil is used in commercial cosmetics, shampoos, perfumes, soaps, creams, and skin lotions. From the Greeks and Romans on down, parsley has been used as a handy breath freshener, covering and eliminating other, stronger odors.

As a companion plant, parsley is supposed to repel asparagus beetles and is recommended for planting among tomatoes because it attracts the wasps that parasitize tobacco and tomato hornworms. It has also been claimed that planting it with roses will improve their scent and keep the plants healthier. In the second season, when in bloom, it attracts and feeds a wide variety of pollinators, such as honeybees.

Cultivation

Parsley is a relatively cold-tolerant plant, withstanding some frost in spring or again in autumn. Unless seed is wanted, this biennial is usually grown as an annual crop. Seeds can be sown in the garden when the soil has mellowed, reaching a temperature of about 50°F or warmer, and the weather has begun to moderate in mid-spring. Seeds can be sown about 1/4- to 1/2-inch deep in soil that has been finely pulverized to ensure good seed-to-soil contact. The soil should be kept uniformly moist until seedlings appear. To prevent soil crusting which might impair emergence, the seeds can be covered with vermiculite rather than garden soil. If not pre-treated, germination and emergence may occur over a fairly long time, from ten to twenty-four days, because of heraclenol, a coumarin, in the seeds. This chemical can be leached from the seeds by soaking for three days in 77°F water, draining, rinsing, and then sowing. The cooler the soil, the slower the process will progress.

Seed started indoors or in the greenhouse and transplanted into pots or cell packs will germinate more quickly and uniformly. Bottom heat will also speed the process. Due to weed pressure in the garden, this method may be preferable because it avoids weeds having a head start on the plants and also allows precision spacing of the plants. When properly hardened off, these transplant from pots or cell packs very well, with little root disturbance.

Best soil for parsley is a well-drained, fertile garden loam, with high humus and water-holding capacity. Parsley is tolerant of pH levels from 5.3 to 7.3 (acid to somewhat alkaline.) Added fertilizer should be in either a 1-1-1 or 3-1-2 ratio of nitrogen, phosphoric acid, and potash, similar to that for growing other green, leafy vegetables. Compost or other organic materials can be used to improve soil texture and water retention. Mulching will even out soil temperature and moisture for best growth. Full sun exposure is best, but they will tolerate some shade, with at least six hours of sun exposure each day.

Once fully established, the outer leaves may be harvested by cutting back to near the rosette, taking care not to damage the growing point in the center of the rosette. In commercial fields, mature plants are harvested by cutting all the foliage back to within an inch or two of the crown. After heavy harvest, a side dressing of nitrogen will speed regrowth and repeat harvest. Irrigate as necessary to keep soil moist but not waterlogged.

Especially with direct-seeded plants, but also with young transplants, weed control is essential as early growth of parsley plants is quite slow, because nutrient reserves in the tiny seeds is minimal. Once the taproot gets established, the plants become much more robust. Although established parsley plants exhibit a bit of allelopathy, inhibiting growth of nearby plants, careful and timely weeding will still be necessary all through the growing season. Mulching with organic or other materials will help keep weed growth to a minimum.

Parsley does well in window boxes, pots, or other containers and can be brought inside and grown on a sunny windowsill throughout the winter. High light and relatively cool temperatures are best for indoor culture. Discard overwintered plants in spring and start over with new plants. Growing in a cold frame will extend the fall harvest season, as will floating row covers.

If a few plants are allowed to overwinter in the garden to flower and set seeds, they may reseed themselves. In cooler climates, these overwintering roots may need a thick protective mulch to guarantee survival through winter. If subjected to 30 or more days of temperatures below 40°F, plants may flower in the first growing season, so setting the plants in the garden too early in the spring should be avoided.

There are many cultivars of both the curled and flat leaf varieties of parsley. Curled selections include 'Banquet', 'Curlina', 'Deep Green', 'Forest Green', 'Moss Curled', and 'Sherwood'. Flat leaf cultivars might include 'Argon', 'Perfection', 'Plain', and 'Plain Italian Dark Green'. In Italy, the cultivar known as 'Catalogno' is considered the true Italian parsley. When it is available in the U.S., it is usually listed as 'Giant Italian'. The Hamburg or Parsnip Rooted cultivars include 'Arat', 'Berliner', 'Fakir', 'Hamburg', 'Halblange', 'Hilmar', and 'Sugar', although 'Hamburg' is by far the easiest to find. Root types should be direct sown to avoid disfiguring the roots.

Pests and Diseases

Damping off, caused by *Pythium* species fungus, can be a problem with seeds sown indoors or in the greenhouse. These can be pretreated with a fungicide to prevent disease development. Using sterile planting medium and sterilized flats or cell packs for seed starting will eliminate those sources of infection. Also, avoid overcrowding, overwatering, and poor air circulation to minimize the danger from this disease. Having a fan to move air over the developing seedlings can sometimes be all that is needed to prevent this problem.

Parsley plants are also susceptible to crown rot if plants are overwatered or periodically inundated by natural rain. Planting on raised beds or ridges, or amending the soil to improve internal drainage can help to avoid this condition.

A variety of insects may sometimes feed on parsley plants and need to be controlled if severe damage occurs. These might include aphids, cabbage loopers, beet armyworms, carrot weevils, corn earworms, flea beetles, leafhoppers, and tarnished and other plant bugs. The caterpillar larvae of the black swallowtail butterfly can quickly defoliate plants in this family. Look for black and green striped caterpillars with yellow dots, which will feed on the plants for two weeks, then pupate and eventually emerge as adult butterflies. These can be controlled with sprays, hand picking, or if other Apiaceae plants are growing in abundance, such as wild carrot or wild parsnip, one can pick these off and relocate them to these other acceptable hosts, saving the garden plants. In most locales, the black swallowtail butterfly is not endangered because of the abundance of acceptable hosts, so controlling them on parsley, dill, or fennel will not adversely affect the overall population of these beautiful butterflies.

Parsley has been used to attract rabbits and hares, which prefer this plant over all others. Where these animals are numerous, protection may be necessary to prevent heavy herbivory. When in flower, parsley attracts bees and other nectar-feeding insects. Birds such as goldfinches love to feed on the seeds.

Harvesting

Once established, plants can be harvested regularly, either by removing outer leaves from the rosette down near the crown, or by cutting the whole plant back to about an inch. It all depends on whether a little is needed at a time, or a larger amount all at once. Commercial operations may harvest multiple times by this drastic method with good results. Nitrogen and water are all that are required to spring the plant back to fast growth. In the home garden, the former method is usually practiced unless a large batch of parsley pesto is on the menu. With this gradual method, harvest can continue all season, without undue stress on the plants.

Store fresh parsley in the refrigerator in a perforated plastic bag. Wash thoroughly, to remove sand and soil particles, then pat dry and place in the plastic bags. If it is wilted after harvest, washing should restore some of the moisture it needs to maintain quality. If properly prepared, it should last a week or so in the crisper drawer.

In some areas, parsley has naturalized and grows wild. Extreme caution should be exercised when attempting to harvest these wild plants because several similar-looking plants from the same family are deadly poisonous. These include *Aethusa cynapium*, fool's parsley; *Conium maculatum*, poison hemlock; and *Cicuta maculata*, water hemlock. All three are capable of causing death if ingested. One should either become an expert botanist who can correctly identify these plants 100 percent of the time, or grow or purchase parsley and avoid wildcrafting.

Preservation

Parsley's quality and flavor are much better fresh than dried. Fresh frozen is also preferable to dried, although freeze-drying can maintain fresh quality in the dried product as long as it is sealed to prevent oxidation. Freshly chopped parsley can be frozen with water in ice cube trays which can then be dropped into a dish that is being prepared. Crispness is destroyed by freezing, but taste remains fairly intact.

If parsley is to be dried, it should be done in the shade, as quickly as possible.

It may need to be finished in either a food dehydrator or oven on the lowest setting to accomplish this. Heat drives off the essential oils that flavor the plant material. Parsley may also be dried in the oven or dehydrator from beginning to end, just taking care to heat it as little as necessary to dry it quickly, which will preserve both the color and some of the flavor of the dried product. Once dried, it should be crushed and stored in an airtight container, away from moisture and light. Flat leaf types may dry more effectively than curly ones.

Summary

Parsley is a deserving International Herb Association Herb of the Year™ for a variety of reasons. For too long, parsley has been taken for granted by too many people. While it is appreciated in the cuisine of many places around the world, parsley is still an underdog in the U.S. Its history and lore are varied and quite interesting. It has long been cultivated and utilized in a variety of ways. Medicinally, it has many proven values and a few more fanciful ideas of efficacy. A culinary workhorse, parsley plays very well with other herbs and flavorings, while seldom taking center stage.

Given the difficulty of germinating the seeds and establishing the plants, the crop is otherwise quite easy to grow, and will produce well if protected from rabbits, butterfly larvae, and a few other pests. Once established, it can be harvested either regularly or periodically to have at hand to use in a variety of ways. It can be preserved for later use and stores fairly well. Finally, always remember that the petiole of the leaf is just that and not a "stem," which only elongates and appears in the second year as the plant flowers and sets seed.

References

"All About Parsley." *The Spruce Eats*. https://www.thespruceeats.com/all-about-parsley-2355733. Accessed 6/11/20.

Belsinger, Susan and Arthur O. Tucker. *The Culinary Herbal*. Timber Press, 2016. 187-189.

"Essential Facts for Parsley." *Herb Society of America*. https://herbsocietyorg.presencehost.net/file_download/inline/140a12b8-0fe0-4a52-ac2c-2b61ea6e786a. Accessed 6/11/20.

"Everything You Need to Know About Parsley." *Flat Leaf Parsley*. https://www.flatleafparsley.com/. Accessed 6/11/20.

Foster, Steven and Varro E. Tyler. *Tyler's Honest Herbal*, 4 ed. Hayworth Herbal Press, 1999. 281-282.

"Herb Profile: Parsley." *The Herb Information Site*. https://www.herbinfosite.com/herb-information/herb-profile-parsley/. Accessed 6/11/20.

Hylton, William H., ed. *The Rodale Herb Book*. Rodale Press, 1974. 526-530.

"Information About Parsley." *Gardening Know How*. https://www.gardeningknowhow.com/edible/herbs/parsley. Accessed 6/11/20.

Kowalchic, Claire and William H. Hylton, eds. *Rodale's Illustrated Encyclopedia of Herbs*. Rodale Press, 1987. 407-409.

"Learn About Parsley." *What's Cooking America*. https://whatscookingamreica.net/LizKrause/Parsley.htm. Accessed 6/11/20.

"Parsley: A Popular Herb with a Long History." *Redlands Daily Facts*. https://redlands dailyfacts.com/2015/11/23/parsley-a-popular-herb-with-a-long-history/. Accessed 6/11/20.

"Parsley." *Encyclopedia Britannica*. https://www.britannica.com/plant/parsley. Accessed 6/11/20.

"Parsley Growing and Harvest Information." *Veggie Harvest*. https://veggieharvest.com/herbs/parsley.html. Accessed 6/11/20.

"Parsley: Health Benefits, Facts, and Research." *Medical News Today*. https://www.medicalnewstoday.com/articles/284490. Accessed 6/11/20.

"Parsley." *Specialty Produce, the App.* https://www.specialtyproduce.com/produce/Parsley 325.php. Accessed 6/11/20.

"Parsley." *Wikipedia.* https://en.wikipedia.org/wiki/Parsley. Accessed 6/11/20.

"Parsley." *The World's Healthiest Foods.* http://www.whfoods.com/genpage.php?tname=foodspice&dbid=100. Accessed 6/11/20.

"Petroselinum crispum." *University of Illinois Extension, Herb Gardening.* https://web.extension.illinois.edu/herbs/parsley.cfm. Accessed 6/11/20.

Tucker, Arthur O. and Thomas DeBaggio. *The Big Book of Herbs.* Interweave Press, 2000. 470-474.

"Why Parsley Is Good to Eat." *Better Health Channel.* https://www.betterhealth.vic.gov.au/health/ingredientsprofiles/Parsley. Accessed 6/11/20.

Charles Voigt is a retired faculty member at the University of Illinois at Urbana-Champaign. He was a state vegetable and herb specialist there from 1988 through 2015. In 1989, he was on the steering committee that wrote the bylaws forming the Illinois Herb Association. He first presented a talk at the International Herb Growers and Marketers Association (later renamed International Herb Association or IHA) in 1991. He was head of the host committee for IHA's 1995 conference in Chicago, IL. At the Portland, OR, IHA conference in 2001 he received IHA's Service Award, and in 2010, in Collinsville, IL, their Professional Award. In 2014 in Toronto, he presented the Otto Richter Memorial Lecture at the annual IHA conference. He served on the IHA Program Committee for many years and has been the chair of the Horticulture Committee since 1997. This committee has been instrumental in choosing and promoting Herbs of the Year. Chuck is currently the chair of the IHA Foundation. He also wrote the popular book, *Vegetable Gardening in the Midwest*, with his vegetable mentor, Dr. Joseph Vandemark. One of Chuck's goals in retirement is to sing in 100 gardens, although the current pandemic has put a crimp in that process and he's stalled at seventeen.

To the Devil
Nine Times
and Back

Susan Belsinger

When you were a kid, did you ever play the game where everyone is in a circle and the first person in the circle whispers something in the next person's ear and it is passed around the circle thus so, until the last person says what they heard and it is nothing like what the first person said? Well, doing research for the old saying about the germination time of parsley is pretty similar.

In the first book that I co-authored with Carolyn Dille, *Cooking with Herbs*, we wrote, "Parsley's slow germination has stimulated some fanciful theories: that it goes to the devil nine times and back before it sprouts, or that a pregnant woman planting it speeds germination." During our research back then, from books not the internet, we found this old adage in many different sources.

Upon getting ready to write this article, besides finding variations on this saying in books, I found numerous versions in many places online. In fact, when I first gave our editor of this book my title way back when, she wrote back to me and said, "Are you sure it is nine times and not *seven*?"

In *The Big Book of Herbs* by Arthur O. Tucker and Thomas DeBaggio, my mentors state: "Parsley's slow germination has given rise to the fanciful tale that the seed has to go to Hell nine times and back before it will germinate." I really hoped to find the source for this saying, though I had no luck. And while looking for a source, I came across the following variations.

Oxford Reference at least gives us an idea of when this saying first appeared: "Proverbial saying, mid-17th century, meaning that it is often slow to germinate; there was a superstition that parsley, which belonged to the Devil, had to be sown nine times before it would come up."

According to *World Wide Words.org*, the number nine features heavily in

Parsley for sale under the arbor at the Ozark Folk Center. *Susan Belsinger*

cultural idioms: "There are also the proverbs: possession is 'nine points of the law', 'a stitch in time saves nine' and the old gardening saw that 'parsley seed goes nine times to the devil' before it germinates" (Quinion).

According to *Mysticalnumbers.com*, nine can be a sacred number, a number of magic, the number of heaven, and more. "In England there was a superstition that parsley went nine times to the devil and back before it started to sprout. For this reason it was not appropriate to give a parsley plant as a gift. Naturally it was considered quite unlucky for anyone to receive a gift that had frequently visited the devil."

Here are a few quotes using the number *seven* rather than *nine*. Garden Betty covers her bases with "[P]arsley has to travel to hell and back *seven* times before it will sprout. Some sources actually say *nine* times, so to be safe, you should sow *nine* times as many seeds as you need, since the devil keeps the rest for himself."

In her article "Between the Rows", Pat Leuchtman asserts, "I do not plant parsley from seed because it takes so long to germinate. There is a saying that parsley has to go to Satan and back *seven* times before it will germinate. Buying a flat of plants is easier."

And finally, in this quote from *Nutritional Geography*, we get it all—wives, witches, Good Friday—and your choice of trips to the devil! "It is said that the wife dominates the family if parsley in the garden remains green throughout the year; alternatively, whoever plants parsley and it flourishes will be the head of household; parsley flourishes only when planted by a witch; if parsley in one's garden is needed throughout the year, it must be planted on Good Friday; parsley seeds visit the Devil *three-seven-nine* times before it grows and flourishes …"

Knowing the science and paying attention to experienced herb growers is important. According to Art Tucker and Tom DeBaggio, "[T]he slow germination is due to a high concentration in the seeds of heraclenol, a coumarin, but this is easily leached out with water. Germination will thus be enhanced by soaking the seeds in aerated water for three days at 77°F (25°C), draining, rinsing and then sowing 1/4 inch deep (0.6cm) in a fine seedbed."

This spring, in preparation for Parsley to be celebrated as the 2021 Herb of the Year ™, I soaked my nine cultivars of *Petroselinum crispum* seeds for only 24 hours and my germination was so slow that I calculated all nine trips to the devil and back were about three days each; it took nearly a month for most of them to sprout. Upon discussing this with my neighboring farmer/

herb grower, Denise Sharp of Sharp Farm, she told me that she always soaks her parsley seed for at least three days before sowing. Which I will do for sure, next year!

> This adage of seeds is amusing to contemplate
> Travel time or hot spot is yours to ruminate
> The Devil and Satan are one and the same
> And Hell is the place from whence they came
> Whether it is seven or nine trips, we can speculate
> It is a long time to wait for parsley to germinate.

> —Susan Belsinger

Close-up of parsley seeds. *Susan Belsinger*

References

Belsinger, Susan and Carolyn Dille. *Cooking with Herbs*. Van Nostrand Reinhold Company, 1981.

Leuchtman, Pat. "Between the Rows: What you should know about growing common herbs." *Greenfield Recorder*. https://www.recorder.com/Between-the-Rows-What-you-should-know-about-growing-common-herbs-16067293. Accessed 7/23/20.

Li, Linda. "That Devilish Parsley." *Garden Betty*. https://www.gardenbetty.com/that-devilish-parsley/. Accessed 7/23/20.

"Number 9." *Mysticalnumbers.com*. https://mysticalnumbers.com/number-9/. Accessed 7/20/20.

"Parsley." *Nutritional Geography*. https://nutritionalgeography.faculty.ucdavis.edu/parsley/. Accessed 7/23/20.

"Parsley seed goes nine times to the Devil." *Oxford Reference*. https://www.oxfordreference.com/view/10.1093/oi/authority.20110803100307995). Accessed 7/23/20.

Quinion, Michael. "Nine days wonder." *World Wide Words*. https://www.worldwidewords.org/qa/qa-nin3.htm. Accessed 7/23/20.

Tucker, Arthur O. and Thomas DeBaggio. *The Big Book of Herbs*. Interweave Press, 2000. 470-474.

See bio page 8.

Hamburg Parsley Root. *Deb Jolly*

Hamburg Parsley:
An Herb with Ancient Roots

Bevin Cohen

Parsley is native to the Mediterranean region and boasts a long and fascinating history of uses from celebratory wreaths and tomb decorations to medicinal treatments and, of course, as a garnish alongside meals. There are a handful of varieties available to the herbalist including the traditional curled parsley, *P. crispum* var. *crispum*, and the flat leafed Italian types, *P. crispum* var. *neapolitanum*. These varietals were first brought to North America by Dutch colonists in the early 1600s and they both remain popular as culinary and medicinal herbs today. Unfortunately, one variety of parsley wasn't able to secure this acceptance amongst the populace in the States, although its history is just as significant and its culinary attributes just as appealing. I speak, of course, of the Hamburg Parsley, *Petroselinum crispum* var. *tuberosum*, a varietal grown specifically for its succulent and flavorful taproot.

Although parsley is of Greek descent, it was in northern Germany where this particular variety made its claim to fame, in its namesake town of Hamburg, where the root was enjoyed steamed and mashed much like one would partake of parsnip. In fact, parsley's closest botanical relative in the family Apiaceae is the parsnip (*Pastinaca sativa*) and the roots are quite comparable in appearance and flavor.

Hamburg parsley, also known as turnip-rooted parsley, can be grown in the garden from seed just as one would propagate a curly or flat leafed variety. The leaves of this variety are similar to that of the Italian types, but the flavor of the leaf is slightly more bitter than those traditionally cultivated for their aerial portions. The bitter greens of root parsley can certainly be utilized in a soup stock, as was common practice in 17th century Germany where they were often referred to as a *suppengruns* or soup greens.

Parsley root will be ready to harvest approximately one hundred days after sowing. The crop can be heavily mulched to prevent the ground from freezing in the winter and the roots can be pulled and enjoyed as needed throughout the cold season. The gardener will find that the sweetness of the taproot is enhanced by exposure to a mild frost. In many places parsley grows as a biennial, meaning that it won't flower until its second year. Each plant will produce hundreds of seeds and this herb may certainly reseed itself into the garden.

Although parsley seeds can be quite slow to germinate, allowing the plant to propagate itself this way is often more successful than planting the seeds intentionally. If the gardener does choose to direct-seed their parsley, soaking the seeds overnight and then planting them out a couple weeks before the final frost is highly recommended.

It's important to note that parsley flowers are insect-pollinated and therefore varieties can easily become crossed. This means that the next generation grown from cross-pollinated seed is likely to show a mix of traits, which the gardener may or may not find desirable. For a gardener who would like to keep the extensive taproot trait of the Hamburg parsley variety pure, it is best to only allow this one varietal of parsley to flower at a time, thus ensuring the purity of the seed harvest.

This unique variety of parsley may not be a common find in the gardens of North America but with its flavorful, bitter greens and deliciously edible taproot, Hamburg parsley makes a worthwhile addition to any garden.

Bevin Cohen is an author, herbalist, gardener, seed saver, and educator. He's the owner of Small House Farm and the founder of Michigan Seed Library Network. Cohen offers workshops and lectures across the country on the benefits of living closer to the land through seeds, herbs, and locally grown food, and has published numerous works on these topics, including his most recent book, *The Artisan Herbalist* (New Society Publishers 2021). He serves on the board of the International Herb Association and the advisory council for the Community Seed Network, a multinational education and networking platform. Learn more about Cohen's work on his website, www.smallhousefarm.com.

'Large Leaf' Parsley makes an attractive edging. *Pat Kenny*

Petroselinum crispum var. *neopolitanum* 'Italian Giant' parsley. *Pat Kenny*

Parsleys of the World, Unite!

Kathleen Connole

As we celebrate Parsley, *Petroselinum crispum*, Herb of the Year™ 2021, it is very interesting to discover that there are a number of other plants that are commonly called "parsley." They all resemble in appearance the familiar herb most well-known as parsley.

There are plants from all over the world that are also named parsley. Not only do they look like *Petroselinum crispum*, but they have other qualities in common. Of course, that makes sense since most of them belong to the same family, Apiaceae. The parsley look-alikes often have similar culinary and medicinal uses; however, a few of them are toxic. They are a very prolific bunch and play an important role in attracting insect pollinators, especially swallowtail butterflies. Several of these plants are currently being studied for their potential medicinal value in treating cancer. Except for the toxic members of Apiaceae, these parsleys have provided food, flavor, and medicine for people worldwide, wherever they can be found growing.

The native origins of these parsley look-alikes are primarily in the temperate regions of the world, ranging from wetlands to mountainous regions; some have adapted to dry desert-like climates. A few that have naturalized in areas outside of their original lands are considered invasive, and some have become endangered where they are endemic.

The earliest fossil records of Apiaceae have been found dating back to the late Eocene Epoch, 38 million to 33.9 million years ago. The climate was cooling, polar ice caps were forming, and the continents were drifting apart towards their present positions (Berkeley.edu).

This plant family, consisting of 300 genera and 2500 to 3000 species, was one of the first flowering plants to be systematically classified by plant taxonomists in the late 1600s. In 1672, Scottish botanist Robert Morrison stated that it was "nearly cosmopolitan, found largely in temperate uplands" (Berkeley.edu).

The botanical characteristics of the family Apiaceae, originally known as Umbelliferae, have led to its widespread distribution worldwide. The name comes from the Latin word *umbellula*, for *little shade*. The flowers, known as umbels, are composed of multiple florets clustered in a flat-topped disc, each floret with 5 sepals and 5 petals, making them very attractive to a number of pollinators—flies, mosquitoes, bees, wasps, moths, butterflies, and other insects. These insects, along with the wind, facilitate pollination, including cross pollination between members of the same genus. The numerous biennial members of this family often reseed freely, allowing them to spread easily. The development of fleshy taproots has resulted in many species being an important carbohydrate food source (web.bvu.edu).

The majority of this group of parsleys occur naturally in Europe, including the Mediterranean region, west and central Asia, and northwest Africa. Two exceptions are Chinese Hemlock Parsley, *Conioselinum chinense*, that is native to Russia, the Far East, and northern North America; and Australian or Sea Parsley, *Apium prostratum*, found in Australia and New Zealand. Several are found only in North America, primarily in the western United States and Canada.

Two plants commonly called parsley belong to families other than Apiaceae. Parsley Piert or Field Parsley, *Alchemilla arvensis*, is a member of Rosaceae. Native to Europe, north Africa, and western Asia, it is also called Field Lady's Mantle. It has been introduced into North America and grows at lower elevations than Common Lady's Mantle, *A. vulgaris*, also introduced from Eurasia. The name *Piert* is derived from *piercestone*, as one of its medicinal uses is to treat bladder stones. The genus name *Alchemilla* is derived from *Alkemelych* (alchemy, Arabic) and is said to be either due to its many medicinal virtues, or to the "mystic potions" made including dewdrops collected from the leaves (Grieve, botanical.com). The whole herb, fresh or dried, has been used for centuries in folk medicine as a diuretic and demulcent, to treat dropsy, liver obstructions, jaundice, bladder and kidney ailments. It is interesting to note that *Petroselinum crispum* is also used for bladder and kidney issues.

Parsley fern, *Cryptogramma crispa*, is a true fern, in the *Pteridaceae* family; its leaves resemble those of common parsley. However, it is not used for medicinal or culinary purposes. This plant is native to the boreal-montane regions of Europe and can be found growing on steep slopes, cliffs, and stone walls. Scientific studies have been done of the cuticular waxes of parsley fern, of interest due to the plant's ability to protect itself from UV radiation, insects, pathogens, and evaporative water loss. American parsley fern, *C. acrostichoides*, can be found growing in "massive tufts" in the Pacific

Northwest (hardyferns.org).

The plants known as parsleys that are native to the Old World include several that contain toxic chemicals. Fool's or Poison Parsley, *Aethusa cynapium*, originating in Europe, West Asia, and Northwest Africa, can be found growing in waste places and cultivated ground. It has been introduced in other parts of the world and was used historically in folk medicine for gastrointestinal problems, especially in children; it is a stomachic and sedative. The active component is the alkaloid cynopine, toxic, but less so than its extremely poisonous relative, Poison Hemlock, *Conium maculatum*, also commonly called Poison Parsley.

Wild Parsley, *Oenanthe peucidanifolia*, grows in the wet grasslands of the same regions and is said to contain psychotropic properties. This genus contains several other very poisonous plants. Milk Parsley, also called Hog Fennel, *Peucedanum palustre*, is native to Europe and central Asia, where it prefers fens, marshes, and calcareous soils. This so-called parsley is a host plant to the Old World swallowtail butterfly. It too contains the psychotropic substance myristicine. The name *milk parsley* refers to the sap, a milk-like latex which can cause photosensitivity if it contacts the skin. The root of Milk Parsley was referred to as an anticonvulsant in the 1800s by British botanist John Lindley. Two other toxic parsley look-alikes to beware of, *Cicuta maculata*, Water Hemlock or False Parsley, and *Heracleum mantegazzianum*, Giant Hogweed or Giant Cow Parsley, are discussed elsewhere in this book.

The remainder of the Old World plants with parsley in their common names include those with culinary and/or medicinal uses. This list is the most numerous, containing 10 or more members of Apiaceae.

Cow or Wild Beaked Parsley, *Anthriscus sylvestris*, inhabits roadsides, fields, and woodland edges in Europe and Asia. It has been introduced into North America and can be weedy and invasive. It closely resembles Poison Hemlock; note that the stem is hairy, rather than smooth like its poison relative, but the leaves and roots are edible. The leaves can be cooked or eaten raw, and the root is cooked. According to the website *Plants for a Future*, the leaves "taste somewhat less than wonderful". The fruits have been used as a spice for cheese since antiquity. The leaves and stems can be used to make a beautiful green dye. Many sources cite a multitude of medicinal uses, including some that are common to other wild Apiaceae species. Traditional applications include "a tonic for general weakness" (pfaf.org); for headache; as antitussive, antipyretic, analgesic, diuretic, anti-inflammatory, antiviral and antimicrobial. This plant has also been studied for possible anti-cancer properties. This attribute and the ease of growing it in abundance could make

False Parsley or Water Hemlock, *Cicuta maculata. Fritzflohrreynolds*

it a valuable resource in treating cancer.

Bur or Hedgehog Parsley, *Caucalis platycarpos*, has a similar range as the previous relatives described. This plant will grow in waste places, arable fields, and chalky soils. Introduced into North America, Russia, South Africa, and South America, it too can be weedy and is listed as an invasive. The leaves are eaten raw, cooked as a potherb, or pickled for winter use in salads. Traditional Iranian medicine uses above-ground parts for the antioxidant, antibacterial, and anti-inflammatory qualities. The anti-cancer constituents have been examined and are promising.

Chinese Parsley, *Coriandrum sativum*, is so well known today for the leaves, popular in Mexican and Asian dishes, that some are unaware that its fruits have been used as a spice since ancient times in the Mediterranean, Southern Europe, and Western Asia, where it originates. Seeds have been found in Neolithic excavations. The spice coriander has antioxidant, diuretic, vasodilator, hypolipidemic, carminative, digestive, anti-allergenic, and antibiotic properties, and has been used to treat anxiety, insomnia, and eye disorders. The leaves, named cilantro by the Spanish, also have many health benefits, as they are rich in vitamins, minerals, antioxidants, and can help lower cholesterol, blood pressure, and blood sugar, remove heavy metals from the body, and improve digestion and brain function (healthline.com).

Once coriander was brought to the Americas, it was made use of by various indigenous peoples. The Hopi use the leaves as flavoring in stews, and as a salad green; the Zuni eat the leaves fresh; the Zuni and Keresan use the seeds as a spice to flavor soups and stews, ground and added to chile peppers. The leaves have become a favorite herb of the native peoples of Central and South America. How did it come to be called Chinese Parsley? According to englishstackexchange.com, it was first given that name in 19th century New York, where it was grown by a Chinese immigrant on his vegetable farm. This plant was the IHA Herb of the Year™ in 2017 and the book devoted to its study has much more information on botany, cultivation, folklore, medicinal uses and wonderful recipes.

Next on this list is our 2021 Herb of the Year™ Parsley, *Petroselinum crispum*. The reader will find extensive information about this very nutritious and medicinal herb throughout this book. Of all the Old World parsleys, this is one of the few for which there are listed ethnobotanical uses by Native Americans. The Cherokee people used both the root and the plant tops medicinally as a gynecological aid, abortifacient, urinary and kidney aid, and for dropsy. The Micmac used it for a "cold in the bladder" (naeb.brit.org).

Lovage or Love Parsley, *Levisticum officinale. 4028mdk09*

Lovage, also called Love Parsley, *Levisticum officinale*, is native to mountain pastures and hedgerows near streams in southern Europe. This perennial is frost hardy and has naturalized in other parts of the world, prefers a sunny, cool climate and moist, rich soil, but is adaptable to part shade and waste places. The common name is said to be due to the Greek and Roman belief that it was an aphrodisiac. The seeds were used in a medieval love potion, and "travelers tucked the leaves into their shoes because of their antiseptic and deodorizing properties" (theguardian.com).

Lovage has been used since ancient times for food and medicine. Like other Mediterranean herbs, lovage was brought to the British Isles during the Roman Empire, and from there taken to North America by colonists. All parts are useful, and it was much favored for its hardiness and robust growth habit—it can reach 7 feet in height! The flavor is celery-like, although stronger; the leaves can be used in soups, stews, and salads—it goes especially well with potatoes; and the seeds can be used as a spice, similar to fennel. Hugh Fearnley-Whittingstall, columnist for *The Guardian*, writes of another use: "Use the hollow stem as a peppery, tongue-tingling stirrer for a bloody mary" (theguardian.com). It is said that Queen Victoria carried lovage-flavored candies in a special pocket sewn into her skirts (herbsocietyblog.wordpress.com).

All parts of lovage have medicinal uses: roots and fruits are diuretic, stimulant, carminative; the infused leaves can be used as an emmenagogue, for digestion, as an antiseptic, poulticed to treat boils, and in the bath for skin disorders. The quercetin that it contains is anti-inflammatory and antioxidant. Like other members of Apiaceae, this plant attracts many insect pollinators, including the parasitic wasp that eats tent caterpillars. It seems that lovage fell out of favor and is not well known today, but those who have become familiar with it have found that there is a lot to love about lovage!

Stone Parsley, *Sison amomum*, is native to Southern Europe, the Mediterranean, Asia Minor, and Algeria. The preferred habitat is hedgerows, banks, rough scrubby grasslands, roadsides, disturbed ground, neutral to calcareous soils, and it tolerates sticky clay. The root is cooked and has a celery-like flavor. The leaves and seeds are used as condiments, although according to the website temperatetheferns.info, "the whole plant gives off the rather unusual smell of petrol" and the fresh seeds smell "nauseous". Stone parsley is known to be carminative, diuretic, and diaphoretic.

Alexanders or Horse Parsley, *Smyrnium olusatrum*, has spread from its origins in parts of Europe and Asia and become naturalized in Great Britain since it was introduced in Roman times. It can be found growing in semi-shaded

Horse Parsley, *Smyrnium olusatrum*.
Roger Culos

or sunny, moist woodland edges, or lowland seaside areas. The leaves and young shoots are eaten raw in salad or cooked in soups and stews. The flavor is celery-like but more pungent; it was once more widely cultivated but has been replaced by celery, *Apium graveolens*, since the 15th century. The root is more tender if kept cool over the winter and is eaten cooked. The spicy seeds are used as a black pepper substitute. Medicinal properties are as a bitter, digestive, and diuretic; for asthma, menstrual problems, and wounds, and to boost immunity.

Field Hedge Parsley, *Torilis arvensis*, has been introduced into much of North America from Europe. Also found growing in East Asia and North Africa, it is weedy and not only self-seeds easily but has bristly seeds that cling to fur and clothing, which aids in its dispersal. The favored habitats are roadsides, disturbed areas, and recently cleared woodlands. It is considered an invasive in Texas, Indiana, and California. *Torilis arvensis* subsp. *neglecta* has been used in the Middle East as folk medicine for gastrointestinal illness and for its antimicrobial, antibacterial, and antioxidant properties. It is being studied there as a possible treatment for fighting cancer. *Torilis leptophylla*, also known as Hedge Parsley, has been used similarly in that region and has been found to be a free radical scavenger and cytoprotective.

Another species of *Torilis, T. japonica*, Japanese Hedge Parsley, from Europe and Asia, introduced into North America, shares the same ease of proliferation as *T. arvensis* and can be found growing on roadsides, in fields and waste areas. This aggressive weed can threaten natural woodlands and savannas and is on the invasive list in many parts of the United States. This *Torilis* has been used in Chinese Traditional Medicine for the treatment of hemorrhoids, spasms, uterine tumors, fever, and dysentery. The chemical constituent *torilin*, found in the fruits, has been found to inhibit tumor development, specifically showing favorable results in the treatment of prostate cancer.

Australian or Sea Parsley, *Apium prostratum*, is indigenous to Australia and New Zealand and is also called Sea Celery, as its leaves have a celery-like aroma. True to its common name, it inhabits coastal areas, brackish swamps, and saline riverbanks. This member of Apiaceae is the same genus as celery, *Apium graveolens*. It was eaten by the natives of New Zealand, has a salty,

Australian or Sea Parsley, *Apium prostratum. Marcia Stefani*

celery-like flavor, and became an important vegetable for early explorers and colonists. Written records of Captain Cook's voyages state that the Captain had his crew gather it and bring on board; they boiled it and drank the cooking water to prevent scurvy (nzetc.victoria.ac.nz).

Chinese Hemlock Parsley, *Conioselinum chinense*, is unusual in that its native range includes Russia, China, Japan, Canada, and the northern United States. This plant prefers moist areas such as stream banks, swamps, seeps, fens, and riparian forests. It has been classified as an endangered wetland plant in Illinois, Indiana, Massachusetts, New Jersey, North Carolina, Pennsylvania, and Wisconsin. The Micmac and Malecite aboriginal people of North America used a root infusion, in combination with some other herbs, as a urinary aid. Pacific Hemlock Parsley, *Conioselinum gmelenii*, was used by the Aleut people as a leaf infusion for colds and sore throats. The Kwakiutl used it in steam baths for arthritis, rheumatism, and "general weakness". The roots were eaten by the Haihais, Haisla, Hanaksiala, Heiltzuk, Kitasoo, Kwakwaka'wakw, Nuxalkmc, and Oweekeno. Another species of *Conioselinum*, Rocky Mountain Hemlock Parsley, *C. scopularum*, was food and medicine for the Navajo and Kayenta. Leaves were cooked with meat. The plant was "smoked for catarrh" and used as a postpartum blood purifier and snake bite remedy (naeb.brit.org).

The last four members of Apiaceae commonly called parsleys are native to North America exclusively. They inhabit a wide range of climates including desert, scrub woodland, prairie, savanna, and montane.

The genus *Cymopterus* can be found in the western United States north to Canada, on hillsides and desert plains up to 6500 feet elevation. There are some 50 different species that belong to this genus. It is unique in this family for having a very low growth habit, with the flower stalks growing sideways. The blooms also are different, as they are thin, whitish, paper-like bracts with numerous small pink to purple florets forming the umbel. There are several species with traditional medicinal and culinary uses. Plains Spring Parsley, *Cymopterus acaulis*, was used as an herb to flavor meats, soups, stew, and cornmeal mush by the Apache, Chiracahua, Navajo, and Mescalero. The shoots and roots were eaten raw by the Comanche, Keres, and Navajo. *C. bulbosus*, Bulbous Spring Parsley, was used as a vegetable (it has a celery-like flavor) by the Acoma, Cochiti, and Laguna. The Navajo and Ramah ate the root raw or roasted and dried it for winter use. The Keres used it as a remedy for stomach ailments, and the Navajo and Ramah as "life medicine". The roots of *C. globulus*, Globe Spring Parsley, were made into a decoction by the Paiute for use as an insecticide. Longstalk Spring Parsley, *C. longipes*, leaves were boiled for food. The seeds and roots of Mountain Spring Parsley,

Widewing Spring Parsley, *Cymopterus purpurascens. Curtis Clark*

C. montanus, were used for food by the Navajo and Gosiute; roots were eaten raw or baked, and dried and stored for winter, then ground for use as a cornmeal substitute. The roots of *C. multinervatus*, Purple Nerve Spring Parsley, were eaten in spring by the Hopi. The specific epithet *multinervatus* means *many veins*. Hopi children ate the roots of Sweetroot Spring Parsley, *C. newberryi*, and the Navajo and Kayenta ate the greens with meat and made an infusion of this plant to treat wounds. These same people made use of Widewing Spring Parsley, *C. purpurascens*, as a potherb to season cornmeal mush and soup; medicinally as an analgesic for backache, an emetic "to settle the stomach after vomiting from swallowing a fly" (naeb.brit.org); and ceremonially in paint for prayer sticks.

Lomatium is the largest genus of Apiaceae that occurs in North America; it contains an incredible number of species and inhabits the western United States and Canada. Many species were used for food and medicine by the native peoples of these regions. There are 34 species of *Lomatium* that include "parsley" in their common names; the majority have "Desert Parsley" as part of their name. More than a few *Lomatium* were called "Biscuit Root", since "the root could be peeled, dried, and ground into flour to make sweet-tasting biscuits" (encyclopedia.com). *Lomatium cous*, Yellow Biscuitroot, was mentioned by the Lewis and Clark Expedition in reference to "root bread" made from the dried and ground root of this plant and obtained through trade with the natives (lewis-clark.org).

Lomatium bicolor var. *leptocarpum*, Wasatch Desert Parsley, roots were eaten fresh and dried for winter use by the Paiute. *L. graveolens* var. *graveolens*, King Desert Parsley, was used as medicine by the Gosiute as a root decoction for colds; the plant was mashed and used as a poultice for sore throats. *L. simplex* var. *simplex*, Great Basin Desert Parsley, roots were eaten in spring and dried and ground into flour by the Montana. Watson's Desert Parsley, *L. watsonii*, was used in the same way by the Paiutes and Oregon people; they cooked it into a mush and used it "to flavor dried crickets" (naeb.brit.org). *L. mohavense*, Mohave Desert Parsley, is a host plant for the Anise and Indra Swallowtail Butterflies. Many other *Lomatium* species are commonly called parsleys; and it is likely that they were also used for food and medicine, although they are not listed in the naeb.brit.org database.

Prairie Parsley, *Polytaenia nuttallii*, is native to the upper Midwest, central and south-central United States. It is listed as endangered and may be extinct in its northernmost range. Considered an indicator plant for original, high quality prairie, this plant prefers a sunny, mesic to dry climate, and the loamy, rocky, or sandy soil found in prairies, plains, savannas, limestone glades, and open woods. The seeds are slow to germinate, requiring 120 days of winter dormancy, and the new plants are also slow to develop. Occasional wildfires that remove competing brush and debris may help facilitate germination.

Nuttall's Prairie Parsley, *Polytaenia nuttallii*. *S.R. Turner*

Once established it will grow a long taproot. The Black Swallowtail Butterfly favors Prairie Parsley as a host plant and many pollinator insects are attracted to the nectar. Grazers will browse on the non-toxic foliage. The winged seeds are dispersed somewhat by wind and were made into a tea for treating diarrhea by the Mesquaki people. *P. texana*, Texas Prairie Parsley, can be found growing from Texas to Oklahoma in rocky limestone soils and attracts the same pollinators including the Black Swallowtail. Native people used the seeds to treat diarrhea.

Mountain or Alpine Parsley, or False Spring Parsley, *Pseudocymopterus montanus*, is endemic to the western United States. True to its name, it prefers an altitude from 6000 to 14,000 feet and can be found growing in aspen groves, woodlands, forest clearings, meadows, and on rocky slopes. The Navajo and Kayenta used the entire plant as a ceremonial emetic; the Navajo and Ramah made an infusion or decoction for use as a gastrointestinal remedy. The leaves were eaten as a green by the Hopi; the Navajo and Ramah cooked the greens with cornmeal, and the stout taproot was cooked with meat.

I would like to thank Pat Kenny for the idea of writing about the many plants called parsley, and for doing the initial research to compile a list of their common and botanical names. I had no idea there would be so many—I even found some to add to her list—and it was fascinating to learn about their origins, uses, differences, and similarities to Parsley, *Petroselinum crispum*, Herb of the Year 2021.

References

"*Aethusa cynapium*, Fool's Parsley: Natural History." *National Center for Homeopathy.* https://www.homeopathycenter.org/medicine_finder/aethusa. Accessed 5/28/20.

"*Alchemilla arvensis* (field parsley piert), *Torilis arvensis*, spreading hedge parsley." *United States Department of Agriculture Natural Resources Conservation Service.* https://www.plants.usda.gov/core/profile?symbol=APAR2 (symbol=TOAR). Accessed 5/28/20.

"*Anthriscus sylvestris* (Wild Chervil or Cow Parsley)." *Minnesota Wildflowers: a field guide to the flora of Minnesota.* https://minnesotawildflowers.info/flower/wild-chervil. Accessed 6/5/20.

"*Apium prostratum, Sison amomum*." *Useful Temperate Plants.* https://

temperate.theferns.info/plant/Apium+prostratum.(Sison+amomum).
Accessed 5/28/20.

"Biscuitroots, *Lomatium, A-Sáblal, Sap-Líl.*" *Discovering Lewis & Clark.*
https://www.lewis-clark.org/article/2408. Accessed 11/20/20.

"*Caucalis platycarpos*, Carrot Bur Parsley." *Global Biodiversity
Information Facility.* https://www.gbif.org/species/303453. Accessed
6/7/20.

"*Conioselinum chinense*, Chinese Hemlock Parsley." *Native Plant Trust Go
Botany.* https://gobotany.nativeplanttrust.org/species/. Accessed 11/17/20.

"*Conioselinum chinense*, Hemlock-parsley." *Michigan State University
Extension, Michigan Natural Features Inventory.* https://mnfi.anr.msu.edu/
species/description/13325/Conioselinum-chinense. Accessed 6/7/20.

"*Coriandrum sativum*." *Missouri Botanical Garden Gardening Help.*
https://missouribotanicalgarden.org/PlantFinder/PlantFinderDetails.
aspx?taxonid=275984. Accessed 6/7/20.

"*Cryptogramma acrostichoides*, Parsley Fern." *Hardy Fern Foundation.*
https://hardyferns.org/ferns/cryptogramma-acrostichoides/. Accessed
11/20/20.

"*Cryptogramma crispa*." *Online Atlas of the British and Irish Flora.* https://
www.brc.ac./uk/plantatlas/plant/cryptogramma-crispa. Accessed 6/27/20.

"*Cymopterus bulbosus*, bulbous spring parsley." *SEI Net Arizona-
New Mexico Chapter.* https://swbiodiversity.org/seinet/taxa/index.
php?taxon=Cymopterus+bulbosus. Accessed 6/27/20.

"Eocene Epoch: Tectonics and Paleoclimate." *University of California-
Berkeley Museum of Paleontology.* https://ucmp.berkeley.edu/tertiary/eoc/
eoctect.html. Accessed 11/17/20.

Facciola, Stephen. *Cornucopia II, A Source Book of Edible Plants.*
Kampong Publications, 1998.

Fearnley-Whittingsall, Hugh. "Hugh Fearnley-Whittingsall's lovage
recipes." June 24. 2011. *The Guardian.* https://theguardian.com/
lifeandstyle/2011/jun24/lovage-recipes-hugh-fearnley-whittingsall.
Accessed 11/20/20.

Gleason, Henry A. and Arthur Cronquist. *Manual of Vascular Plants of the Northeastern United States and Adjacent Canada*, 2 ed. New York Botanical Garden, 1991.

Grieve, Mrs. M. "Lady's Mantle." *A Modern Herbal*. 1931. *Botanical.com, Home of the electronic version of "A Modern Herbal" by Maude Grieve, originally published in 1931*. https://www.botanical.com/botanical/mgmh/l/ladman05.html. Accessed 11/20/20.

Guo, Uanjun and Jia Jun Li, Lucas Busta, Reinhard Jetter. "Coverage and composition of cuticular waxes on the fronds of temperate ferns *Pteridium aquilinum, Cryptogramma crispa, Polypodium glycyrrhiza, Polystichum munitum,* and *Gymnocarpium Dryopteris.*" *Annals of Botany*, September 2018. https://www.ncbi.nih.gov/pmc/articles/PMC6153475/. Accessed 6/27/20.

Hedrick, U.P., ed. *Sturtevant's Edible Plants of the World*. Dover Publications, 1972.

"How Did Chinese Parsley Get Its Name?" *English Language and Usage*. https://english.stackexchange.com/questions/363647/how-did-chinese-parsley-get-its-name. Accessed 11/20/20.

"Introduction to the *Apiales*, carrot-kin." *University of California-Berkeley Museum of Paleontology*. https://ucmp.berkeley.edu/anthophyta/asterids/apialesfr/html. Accessed 11/17/20.

"Invasive Species: *Torilis japonica*, Japanese Hedge Parsley." *USDA Cooperative Extension Invasive Species*. https://invasive-species.extension.org. Accessed 11/17/20.

Johnson, Jackie. "Learning to Love Lovage." *The Herb Society of America Blog*. https://herbsocietyblog.wordpress.com/2017/07/06/3703/. Accessed 11/17/20.

Lawton, Barbara Perry. *Parsleys, Fennels, and Queen Anne's Lace: Herbs and Ornamentals From the Umbel Family*. Timber Press, 2007. 152-156.

"Lewis and Clark Expediton." *Encyclopedia.com*. https://www.encyclopedia.com/history/united-states-and-canada/us-history/lewis-and-clark-expedition. Accessed 11/20/20.

"*Lomatium*." *Native American Ethnobotany Database*. https://www.naeb.brit.org/uses/search/?string=Lomatium+. Accessed 10/15/20.

Mabberly, David J. *Mabberly's Plant-Book*. Cambridge University Press, 2017.

Moerman, David E. *Native American Ethnobotany*. Timber Press, 1998.

"Mohave Desert Parsley, *Lomatium mohavense*." *California Native Plant Society*. https://calscape.org/Lomatium-mohavense-0. Accessed 10/15/20.

"*Oenanthe peucidanifolia, Smyrnium olusatrum*." *Plants For a Future*. https://pfaf.org/user/Plant.aspx?LatinName=Smyrnium+olusatrum. (Oenanthe+peucidanifolia). Accessed 11/17/20.

Oliver, W.R.B. *Botanical Discovery in New Zealand: The Visiting Botanists*, 1950. *New Zealand Electronic Text Collection*, 2007. https://nzetc.victoria. ac.nz/tm/scholarly/metadata-yei-OliVisi.html. Accessed 11/17/20.

Panoff, Lauren, MPH, RD. "8 Surprising Health Benefits of Coriander." Sept. 17, 2019. *Healthline*. https://healthline.com/nutrition/coriander-benefits. Accessed 11/20/20.

"*Polytaenia nutallii*, Prairie Parsley." *Photographs and Descriptions of the Vascular Plants of Missouri*, USA. https://www.missouriplants.com/ Polytaenia_nuttallii_page.html. Accessed 10/15/20.

"Pseudocymopterus montanus." *Colorado Wildbuds*. https://www. coloradowildbuds.com/wildflowers-by-color/yellow-orange/ pseudocymopterus-montanus/. Accessed 10/15/20.

"*Umbelliferae*: The Parsley Family." *Buena Vista University*. https://web. bvu.edu/faculty/hampton/taxonomy/Umbelliferae/Umbelliferae.htm. Accessed 11/17/20.

Uphof, J.C. *Dictionary of Economic Plants*, 2 ed. Lubrecht & Cramer, Ltd., 1968.

Sweetroot Spring Parsley, *Cymopterus newberryi. Jacob W. Frank*

Kathleen Connole joined the Ozark Folk Center's Heritage Herb Garden team in 2006. Before moving to Buffalo River Country in 2005, Kathleen earned a degree in Plant Science from the University of Missouri–Columbia and worked at Powell Gardens and Farrand Farms in Kansas City, Missouri. She practiced plant propagation and all aspects of greenhouse growing, and artistic gardening in the designing of premier mixed containers.

Since she became the Folk Center's Horticulturist, Kathleen's passion has been to research the natural history of the Heritage Herb Garden's diverse collection of plants, both those native to the Ozarks and those from all over the world. She has presented programs at the Ozark Folk Center's annual Herb Harvest Fall Festival on herbs used by the indigenous peoples of the Americas, and stories of the "plant explorers" who traveled the world in search of new plants. Kathleen serves as chair of the Herb Society of America Ozark Unit, headquartered at the Ozark Folk Center State Park, and as secretary for the International Herb Association Board.

The Poetry of Parsley

Gert Coleman

Petroselinum crispum, best known as that bright green herb sprinkled over culinary offerings, has a celebrated place in literature as well as the kitchen, boudoir, and apothecary. Symbolic of festivity and celebration, parsley is surprisingly associated with death and darkness. Ancient Romans knew it as a symbol of protection and tucked a sprig into their togas to ward off evil and added it to plates to prevent contamination. From Peter Rabbit to the Parsley Massacre, this versatile plant enhances the cultural underpinnings of poetry and beyond. Looking at the deeper, symbolic associations of parsley, we find much food for thought.

As a culinary herb, parsley is nutritional and refreshingly green, not the main dish but an attractive accent. Similar to its use as a garnish on our plates, parsley plays a supporting role in poetry. In this first example, the image of parsley visually accents the title of Billy Collins' ruminative poem, "I Chop Some Parsley While Listening to Art Blakey's Version of 'Three Blind Mice'" without being any part of the narrative.

Not a jazz fan, I read that poem because parsley caught my eye. Proprietors of Italian pork stores understand parsley's eye appeal. They sprinkle freshly chopped parsley on almost every dish—from meatballs to scungilli to marinated mushrooms—and they all look attractive and delicious. Because of parsley, I have often bought way more prepared foods on impulse than I meant to.

Well known for enhancing the flavor of dishes without overwhelming them, parsley combines nicely with many foods, particularly in layers. In his delicious "Ode to Tomatoes," Pablo Neruda teases our taste buds with images of preparing tomatoes for dinner. Parsley adds a festive note:

> …it is wed
> to the clear onion,
> and to celebrate the union
> we

> pour
> oil,
> essential
> child of the olive,
> onto its halved hemispheres,
> pepper
> adds
> its fragrance,
> salt, its magnetism;
> it is the wedding
> of the day,
> parsley
> hoists
> its flag…

When introducing herbs and spices to children, you can comfortably begin with parsley. Its pleasant, lightly spicy (almost but not quite bland) taste and cheerful demeanor are easily tolerated, and if allowing children (or any new cook) to sprinkle parsley on a dish, they really can't overdo it (unlike, say, capsicum or tarragon).

Parsley's curly leaves draw children's attention, a delightfully tactile experience. "Finding Serendipity," a short poem about favorite foods by Angelica Banks, cites parsley as an essential and familiar ingredient:

> Figs are delicious with soft cheese and ham,
> Toast is quite scrumptious with butter and jam,
> Eggs are improved by parsley and salt,
> But milkshakes are best with strawberries and malt.

Celebrated for its medicinal qualities, parsley freshens breath, eases indigestion, and comforts an upset tummy. Cats and dogs will thrive if a little fresh chopped parsley is added to their bowls. In Eastern Europe, farmers once added parsley to the cow's feed around Midsummer Eve (June 24, 25, and 26) to protect them from witchcraft. Stallions were fed parsley to increase stamina and sexual prowess.

Rabbits, hares, and voles adore it and can wipe out your parsley patch overnight. Gardeners have traditionally planted strongly scented herbs like lavender, bee balm, mint, garlic, rosemary, sage, thyme, and yarrow to discourage both deer and rabbits. Parsley is not always lucky for rabbits, however. German hunters once lured rabbits with a mixture of parsley leaves and seeds, fennel seeds, and breadcrumbs (Arrowsmith 206).

Original illustration of Peter feasting on Mr. McGregor's vegetables.
Beatrix Potter

In the beautifully illustrated "The Tale of Peter Rabbit" (1902), Mrs. Rabbit admonishes her children: "You may go into the fields or down the lane, but don't go into Mr. McGregor's garden: your Father had an accident there; he was put in a pie by Mrs. McGregor." But Peter runs straight to Mr. McGregor's garden and gorges on lettuce, French beans, and radishes. "Then, feeling rather sick, he went to look for some parsley. But round the end of a cucumber frame, whom should he meet but Mr. McGregor!"

Dreadfully frightened, Peter barely makes it out alive, losing his shoes and new blue jacket in the process. Peter was smart enough to seek parsley when feeling nauseated after bolting his greens, but pausing for parsley almost cost him his life. Mrs. McGregor was ready to put him into the stewpot.

Celebrating Parsley as the 2021 Herb of the Year™ has the old folk song "Parsley, Sage, Rosemary, and Thyme" coursing through my head, particularly Simon and Garfunkel's haunting and ethereal version. The second line of each verse, "Parsley, sage, rosemary and thyme" works as a unifying refrain. It's the line we all sing along to, certainly the line we remember.

Parsley, sage, rosemary and thyme. *Alicia Mann*

> Are you going to Scarborough Fair:
> Parsley, sage, rosemary and thyme.
> Remember me to one who lives there.
> She once was a true love of mine.

Resonating with longing and heartache, the lyrics remind us that love is never easy. The depicted romance *seems* reasonable until we read or listen to the lyrics carefully. Seeming to negotiate, the lovers alternate, making impossible, fairytale-like demands of each other:

> Tell her to make me a cambric shirt:
> Parsley, sage, rosemary and thyme;
> Without no seams nor needle work,
> Then she'll be a true love of mine.

> Ask him to find me an acre of land:
> Parsley, sage, rosemary and thyme;
> Between the salt water and the sea-sand,
> For then he'll be a true love of mine.

Even in today's highly industrialized textile industry, no one could make a shirt without seams or needlework. And how can you find a plot of land between the sea and the sand? Since only fulfilling these conditions will prove that person to "be a true love of mine," one wonders if this is a love song after all or a dirge of lost love descending into sarcasm, resentment, and justified rejection.

How do parsley, sage, rosemary and thyme come into it? Plants have always served as medicine, food, clothing, shelter, and psychic symbols for humankind. For centuries, healers have prescribed parsley for indigestion, often called *heartburn*. Magically, parsley was believed to defuse or neutralize bitter emotions. Perhaps the lovers want to dispel the painful atmosphere between them. Parsley might be used to heal a hurting heart, or heartburn.

Sage, pungent and bitter, signifies strength, power, and wisdom, qualities often needed in resolving relationship issues. Fragrant rosemary, associated with remembrance, love, fidelity, and wedding rituals, suggests the good times, the love and affection once held between them, with a hint that love could yet again be faithful. Tiny, heroic thyme signifies love and courage. Ancient Greeks believed thyme could boost confidence, confer courage, and banish the melancholy of an old sadness carried for too long.

Ideally, these herbs signify the qualities needed to mend a broken relationship—courage, love, fidelity, strength, resilience, and honesty. Some sources suggest that the four herbs used together make a love potion. According to Scott Cunningham, parsley provokes lust and promotes fertility, but warns those in love not to cut parsley (*Encyclopedia* 171). Such conflicting associations, typical of many herbal symbols but especially parsley, combined with the lovers' impossible tasks make rekindling this love questionable at best.

Parsley has historically been so closely associated with darkness and death that it is considered a plant of the Devil. The ancient Greeks scattered parsley on graves and used it in funeral rites. Parsley's persnickety seed can take so long to germinate that many gardeners give up and curse the plant as evil. In addition, parsley seed oil can have serious side effects. Like most medicines, it's all about the dose and the part of the plant consumed. Parsley roots are stronger than the leaves and the seeds are the strongest of all.

Parsley seed oil was often rubbed on the scalp to prevent baldness, but ingesting a massive dose of parsley seed oil could cause headaches, dizziness, humming in the ears, and even death (Arrowsmith 205). Parsley seed oil can exacerbate kidney disorders and acute infections. In addition, parsley seed oil can stimulate the uterus to bring on menses or cause a miscarriage. Conversely, small doses after an exhausting birth help tone the uterus and restore balance to the reproductive system. Again, it's all about the dose.

Parsley has a long taproot, so transplant with care. According to legend, transplanting can bring about death and misfortune. One old adage warns, "Only the wicked grow parsley" (*Magical Herbalism* 228). Folks have always looked for signs or omens by which to assess the present and foretell the future, or to explain why unexpected things happen. One Franconian superstition warns that transplanting parsley signifies planting a loved one in the grave. In many regions it is considered unlucky to plant or transplant parsley except on Good Friday, and women who have transplanted parsley can expect to have trouble finding husbands or lovers (198). Transplanting parsley may also cause crop failure. In addition, troublesome parsley has numerous poisonous cousins, many called *deadly parsley* or *poison parsley*. See sidebar page 62.

Herbs were often the subject of rhymes, adages, and admonitions. At first glance, the English saying "Welsh parsley is a good physic" sounds like good advice, but *Welsh parsley* was a synonym for the gallow's rope (*Our Herb Garden*). "To be in need of parsley" meant someone was at death's door, pale, sickly, even cadaverous in appearance, and "Where parsley is grown in the garden, there will be a death before year's end" reinforces parsley's dark imagery (Ourherbgarden.com/parsley). In a brief poem whose title "Further

Reflections on Parsley" is longer than the poem itself, humorist-poet Og Nash (1902-1971) states concisely: "Parsley is gharsley," a play on the wo parsley and ghastly.

Words have power and *how* we pronounce words can reveal origins, social class, economic background, nationality, and even politics. Parsley's name starts with the letter *p* in many languages, soon followed by the sound of *r*: *prezzemolo* (Italian), *perejil* (Spanish), *persil* (French), *perrexila* (Basque), *peterselie* (Dutch), *petersilie* (German), *persilja* (Finnish) and *persli* (Welsh).

Rita Dove's 1983 poem "Parsley" records the darkest poetic example of parsley's association with death, when mispronouncing the word parsley had real life, fatal consequences. The dictator Rafael Trujillo (1891-1961) ordered the massacre of Haitians, who spoke French and Creole but not Spanish, when they could not trill the letter *r* in *perejil*, the Spanish word for parsley. In a genocidal purge that lasted five days in October, 1937, Dominican soldiers and civilians slaughtered over 20,000 Haitians with machetes, bayonets, and rifles.

> El General has found his word: *perejil*.
> Who says it, lives.

Dove opens with the image of the tropical dictator's pet parrot, "its feathers parsley green," in a palace, followed by images of Haitian migrant workers toiling in Dominican sugar cane fields. The poem reinforces parsley's conflicting life-death parsley imagery in the final lines:

> The general remembers the tiny green sprigs
> men of his village wore in their capes
> to honor the birth of a son. He will
> order many, this time, to be killed
>
> for a single, beautiful word.

Whether worn as a chaplet to prevent inebriation at parties, drunk to ease digestion, or spread over graves to celebrate the dead, parsley has worked for centuries as a symbol of the best and worst in humankind.

Beware of poisonous parsleys!

Parsley's association with evil and the Devil may be linked to its highly toxic relatives, many of whom are called *false parsley*, *poisonous parsley*, *deadly parsley*, or worse. Part of the Apiaceae family, parsley grew wild in Europe for centuries. During spring and early summer, its benign feathery foliage resembles dill, anise, caraway, fennel, coriander, even Queen Anne's Lace, but also some malignant cousins. In 1845, the children of an English tailor, thinking they had gathered parsley, added poison hemlock leaves to their father's sandwich. To everyone's horror, he lurched about drunkenly, became paralyzed, stopped breathing, and died within a few hours (*Wicked Plants* 139).

Ingesting even small amounts of poison hemlock (*Conium maculatum*) can cause motor impairment, weakness, nervous trembling, salivation, lack of coordination, pupil dilation, rapid, weak pulse, convulsions, gastrointestinal irritation, coma, and death (USDA). This tall biennial, listed as a noxious weed in North America, grows along roadsides, in irrigation ditches, and moist waste lots. Its delicate leaves and white taproot initially resemble those of parsley, but as it grows much taller, up to three feet tall, it can be mistaken for Queen Anne's Lace (*Daucus carota*).Whistles made from poison hemlock's hollow stems—marked by purple spots, a notable identifying feature—have caused death in children.

Names are primary symbols of identity and knowing a plant by its Latin or botanic name helps to avoid the confusion of common, folkloric names for plants, particularly since these common names may apply to two or three different plants. **Poison Hemlock**, known as the plant that killed Socrates in ancient Greece, has some telling nicknames: *deadly hemlock, poison parsley, spotted hemlock, European hemlock, California or Nebraska fern*, and, in Scotland, *dead man's oatmeal*. Similarly toxic, **Water Hemlock** (*Cicuta maculata*)— also known as *cowbane, wild carrot, snakeweed, poison parsnip, false parsley, children's bane*, and *death-of-man*—can cause drooling, nausea, vomiting, wheezing, sweating, dizziness, stomach pain, lethargy, delirium, convulsions, heart problems, kidney failure, coma, and death (*WebMD*). A single root, often mistaken for parsnip, can kill a sixteen-hundred-pound cow.

A less toxic but very painful member of parley's extensive family is **Giant Hogweed** (*Heracleum mantegazzianum*), also known as *cartwheel-flower, giant cow parsley, giant cow parsnip*, and *hogsbane*. Featured in the mystery series *Rosemary and Thyme* (S3 E3), giant hogweed contains furanocoumarin derivatives in the leaves, roots, stems, flowers which can cause severe phytophotodermatitis, with oozing blisters and permanent scarring (*Wikipedia*). With so many look-alikes, giant hogweed can be troublesome to identify, and is often confused with cow parsnip (*H. maximum*), poison hemlock, hogweed (*H. sphondylium* and *H. sphondylium ssp sibiricum*), wild parsnip (*Pastinaca sativa*), garden angelica (*Angelica archangelica*), and wild angelica (*A. sylvestris*).

Many of these grow in my fields and, after reading recent county extension bulletins, I have become very cautious about touching any of them. A hellish family, indeed!

Giant Cow Parsley, *Heracleum mantegazzianum*.
Linél

References

Arrowsmith, Nancy. *Essential Herbal Wisdom: A Complete Exploration of 50 Remarkable Herbs*. Llewellyn, 2007. 193-208.

Collins, Billy. "I Chop Some Parsley While Listening To Art Blakey's Version Of 'Three Blind Mice'." *Poem Hunter.com*. www.poemhunter.com/poem/i-chop-some-parsley-while-listening-to-art-blake/. Accessed 10/01/20.

Cunningham, Scott. *Encyclopedia of Magical Herbs*. Llewellyn, 1994. 170-171.

-----. *Magical Herbalism*. Llewellyn, 1995.

Dove, Rita. "Parsley." *Poetry Foundation*. https://www.poetryfoundation.org/poems/43355/parsley. Accessed 6/12/20.

Ghosh, Palash. "Parsley Massacre: The Genocide That Still Haunts Haiti-Dominican Relations." *International Business Times: World*. 10/15/12. www.ibtimes.com/parsley-massacre-genocide-still-haunts-haiti-dominican-relations-846773. Accessed 10/11/20.

"*Heracleum mantegazzianum*." *Wikipedia*. https://en.wikipedia.org/wiki/Heracleum_mantegazzianum. Accessed 10/20/20.

"History of Parsley-Proverbs and Folklore." *Our Herb Garden*. http://www.ourherbgarden.com/herb-history/parsley.html. Accessed 11/23/20.

Neruda, Pablo. "Ode to Tomatoes." *Pablo Neruda Poems*. www.pablonerudapoems.com/ode-to-tomatoes/. Accessed 9/21/20.

Potter, Beatrix. "The Tale of Peter Rabbit." *AmericanLiterature.com*. https://americanliterature.com/author/beatrix-potter/short-story/the-tale-of-peter-rabbit. Accessed 10/01/20.

"Rabbit-Resistant Herbs." *Advice from the Herb Lady*. https://advicefromtheherblady.com/herbs-in-the-garden/garden-helps/rabbit-resistant-herbs/. Accessed 10/23/20.

Rose, Melody. "What is the Significance of Parsley Sage Rosemary and Thyme?" *Dave's Garden*. https://davesgarden.com/guides/articles/view/4394/. Accessed 10/10/20.

"Saying Parsley in European Languages." *In Different Languages*. https://www.indifferentlanguages.com/words/parsley. Accessed 10/27/20.

Stewart, Amy. *Wicked Plants*. Algonquin Books, 2009.

"Why Does the Song 'Scarborough Fair' Say 'Parsley, Sage, Rosemary, and Thyme'?" *Culinary Lore: Food History*. 10/27/12. https://culinarylore. com/food-history:scarborough-fair-parsley-sage-rosemary-thyme/. Accessed 11/2/20.

"Poisonous Plant Research." *USDA Agricultural Research Service*. https:// www.ars.usda.gov/pacific-west-area/logan-ut/poisonous-plant-research/ docs/poison-hemlock-conium-maculatum/. Accessed 10/20/20.

"Water Hemlock." *WebMD*. https://www.webmd.com/vitamins/ai/ ingredientmono-948/water-hemlock. Accessed 10/20/20.

Passionate about herbs, **Gert Coleman** loves, grows, eats, and reads avidly about them. Retired Associate Professor of English at Middlesex County College in New Jersey, she lives on 106 acres in Middlefield, New York, where she and her husband are fixing up another old house, training a new puppy, and planting herbs, flowers, trees, and at-risk native plants. She edited the IHA Herb of the Year™ books (*Cilantro & Coriander*; *Hops: Brewing and Beyond*; *Agastache: Anise Hyssop, Hummingbird Mints and More*; *Rubus*; and *Parsley*), and frequently writes about the legends, lore, and poetry of herbs.

Three times president of the Staten Island Herb Society, she helped to maintain the Colonial Herb Garden at Conference House Park for over 30 years and has started herb gardens at various locations. As a naturalist, she developed and taught parent-tot nature programs at the Staten Island Zoo and local parks, introducing children and adults to local plants, animals, and geology. In addition, she completed a medicinal herbal apprenticeship with internationally acclaimed herbalist Rosemary Gladstar.

Gert is a board member of the International Herb Association and co-chair of the IHA Horticultural Committee; member of the Herb Society of America, North East Herb Association, American Botanical Council, and United Plant Savers. She frequently lectures on various aspects of herbs and teaches workshops on nature writing.

Asafetida in bloom. *www.healthbenefitstimes.com*

Asafetida resin. *Herbalveda.co.uk*

Other Families have Unusual Relatives, Too

Marge Powell

Parsley has a cousin commonly known as asafetida (*Ferula asafoetida*). It is difficult to determine which of the several other spellings for the Latin name—*Ferula asafoetida, F. asa-foetida,* and *F. foetida*—is the preferred one, although the National Center for Biotechnology, U.S. National Library of Medicine, uses *Ferula asafoetida L*. There is not abundant information on this plant, but it raised my curiosity when I was doing research on the local folk medicine of Northeast Florida and Southeast Georgia. Many of the elderly people I interviewed recalled wearing asafetida bags around their necks as children. When I asked why they wore them, I was told, "They were good for everything that might get you sick."

In the early 20th century, areas of Northeast Florida and Southeast Georgia were very rural, and communication was quite limited. So how did a plant that grows in the Middle East enter this local folk medicine tradition? My suspicion is that it traveled with emigrants from Appalachia where asafetida's use was common. But that begs the question, "How did it get to Appalachia?" I cannot answer that question, but I can answer another: "What exactly is asafetida?"

What It Is

Asafetida is the plant pictured to the left.

At first glance, asafetida looks a bit like yellow angelica. According to British herbalist Andrew Chevallier, FNIMH, asafetida is a perennial plant that grows to 6 feet with a massive, fleshy taproot, hollow stem, and compound leaves. It is indigenous to Afghanistan and Iran where it grows at the altitude of two to four thousand feet above sea level on high arid plains

The useful part of the plant is an oleo-gum-resin. The resin is developed from a gum. The gum is produced by harvesting the roots of four-year-old plants, usually in June, that have not yet flowered. The roots are exposed, slashed, then shaded from the sun for five or six weeks. During this time, a gummy liquid leaks out and hardens. When the gummy liquid from the first cut dries, a resin is formed, and another fresh cut is made. The process is continued for about 3 months from the first incision; a single plant may yield up to 1 kilogram of resin before it dries out. The fresh gum is a soft, semiliquid mass that undergoes a gradual color change from shimmering yellowish-white to reddish-brown. The reddish lumps are harvested and are sent to India, Iran, and other countries where they are used both medicinally and culinarily.

The finest product is produced from the leaf bud in the center of the root. According to Maude Grieve, this is called Kandaharre Hing, or *hing*, and is composed of reddish yellow flakes which secrete an oil when squeezed. Chevallier says that the plant secretion is 6 to 17% volatile oil, resin, and gum. This is probably what is exuded when Grieve says the flakes are squeezed. The volatile oil contains about 58% disulphides which play an important protective role for bacteria as a reversible switch that turns a protein on or off when bacterial cells are exposed to oxidation reactions. These disulphides also have an expectorant action and the volatile oil will settle digestion. The resins contain sesquiterpenoid coumarins. Research on the sesquiterpenoid coumarins present in the resins of *Ferula asafoetida* has found them to have antimicrobial, antiprotozoal, and antiviral effects.

Asafetida's Use through Time

The common name *asafetida* is derived from Farsi, a Persian language spoken primarily in Iran, Afghanistan, and Tajikistan. The etymology of asafetida is from the Farsi word *aza* (resin) and the Latin *foetidus* (smelling, fetid). The sulfurous compounds in asafetida give it a distinctive odor and many would say that it stinks. One of its names is Devil's Dung. Many of its historical medicinal claims are a result of the belief that the fetid smell kept germs away. During the Middle Ages, a small piece of the gum was worn around the neck to ward off colds and fevers. Whatever effectiveness it had was probably due to the antisocial properties of the amulet rather than any medicinal virtue.

Asafetida is thought to have been the most popular spice in Ancient Rome. One 4th century Hindu medical treatise declared it to be the best remedy for gas and bloating. In Europe its use has been known since the 12th century. This is the time of the Crusades and it is likely asafetida was brought back to the western world by the Crusaders. And this is my hint of how it journeyed to America. It probably came with European immigrants to the New World.

Asafetida is sometimes applied directly to the skin for corns and calluses, but there is no good scientific evidence to support this use. Today, asafetida is commonly used as a fragrance component in perfumes and in minute quantities in Asian vegetarian cooking. It is also one of the flavorings of Worcestershire sauce.

In magic and mythology, asafetida is used to gain insight and to banish negative energy, evil spirits, and demons. It is used to invoke male gods, especially those of a phallic nature. One myth claims that asafetida developed from the semen of a god of fertility when it soaked into the earth.

In manufacturing, asafetida is used as a flavoring ingredient in foods and beverages. According to WebMD, asafetida is also used in products meant to repel dogs, cats, and wildlife.

Asafetida's Medicinal Use

Asafetida has a long history of medicinal use, especially in India. Because asafetida's volatile oil has components that exit the body via the respiratory system, it aids in the coughing up of congested mucus. This characteristic has caused asafetida to be used for asthma, chronic bronchitis, influenza and other breathing conditions as well as throat problems. Asafetida helps to relieve the spasms in the airways that cause the coughing in the first place. In India it is highly regarded for digestion problems, especially dispelling gas from the stomach and counteracting other spasmodic disorders. Some have found it helpful for Irritable Bowel Syndrome (IBS).

In 1918 asafetida was used in the Spanish influenza pandemic. It was endorsed by the US Pharmacopeia as a remedy for the flu and was stocked by pharmacies for this purpose. The asafetida was worn in a bag, called an acifidity bag, around the neck.

A fluid extract of the resin is taken orally as an emmenagogue by women to restart their periods if menstruation has stopped for some reason. Asafetida excites the secretion of the progesterone hormone. There is evidence that asafetida is an abortifacient and, as such, should be used with extreme caution by anyone who is or suspects she is pregnant. However, it is used extensively in India during and after childbirth. A related species, *Ferula silphion*, was such a highly regarded contraceptive that it was overharvested and became extinct about 300 CE.

Asafetida can be dangerous if administered medicinally to small children. There are documented events that it causes methemoglobinemia, a blood disorder where too little oxygen is carried to the cells.

Ointments containing asafetida are used to repel insects and treat their bites. However, just as the scent of asafetida repels the insects, it may also repel those around you.

Recent studies both pharmacological and biological have shown that asafetida has antioxidant, antiviral, antifungal, antidiabetic, antispasmodic, and hypotensive properties. However, additional studies and clinical trials are needed. A thought that has continued to run through my head as I write this is the applicability of asafetida to the fight against COVID-19. If I were infected, I would use it.

Asafetida's Culinary Use

There is also a long history of the culinary use of asafetida in India and the Middle East. The resin is ground and typically used in many lentil dishes, vegetarian stews and soups, pickles, and some fish dishes. It is also added to dishes that might be difficult to digest or cause flatulence. Some chefs sprinkle a light dusting of the powder on a plate where they will place a freshly grilled steak. It is said to imbue the steak with a savory and unique flavor.

The strong sulfurous odor of asafetida mellows in cooking and provides a strong sweet onion-garlic flavor to dishes. I watched a video (https://www.youtube.com/watch?v=67w296P0SLY) where a chef heated a few tablespoons of oil in a frying pan, then stirred in a few tablespoons of hot peppers and a dusting of asafetida. He swirled the peppers and asafetida in the oil until the peppers wilted. Then he added about two handfuls of kale and a quarter cup of water, covered the pan and cooked until the kale wilted. He uncovered the pan, swirled all the ingredients together again and ate it directly from the frying pan as he exalted the tastiness of the concoction. However, the comments, primarily from ethnic Asian Indians, were unanimous in declaring he overused the asafetida, indicating a pinch, rather than a "dusting" would have been more than adequate.

Asafetida is recommended to people who are unable to digest onions and garlic but want to experience the flavor. Very little of the spice is necessary so a small container lasts a long time. The potent powder is best sautéed in butter (preferably ghee) to dissipate the smell before adding the remaining ingredients to the pot.

The storage of asafetida requires an airtight container enclosed in a sealable bag (or two) to prevent the smell from contaminating other pantry items. Because it is used in such minute quantities in cooking, the culinary use of asafetida is not considered medicinal.

Buyer Beware

Maude Grieve, in her early 20th century herbal, stated that the hing exported to non-Indian markets is often highly adulterated, sometimes with red clay. As a condiment, hing remains an extremely popular flavor in Indian cuisine and is often considered to be good for aiding indigestion. But, contrary to Grieve's assertion that exported hing was likely to be adulterated, today the Indian government is concerned enough about the adulteration in the Indian market that they have published a manual that instructs the consumer on how to detect hing adulteration. It is part of their DART (Detect Adulteration with Rapid Test) program. Three tests for adulteration are explained.

1. <u>Detection of soap, stone or other earthy matter in asafetida (hing)</u>

    a. Shake a little portion of the sample with water and allow to settle.
    b. Pure asafetida will not leave any soap, stone or other earthy matter at the bottom.
    c. If asafetida is adulterated, soap, stone or other earthy matter will settle down at the bottom.

2. <u>Detection of starch in asafetida</u>

    a. Put a sample of the asafetida in a glass of water.
    b. Add tincture of iodine.
    c. If starch is present, blue colored streaks will immediately appear.

3. <u>Detection of foreign resins</u>

    a. Take a spoonful of hing and carefully heat it.
    b. A pure product would burn like camphor, whereas an adulterated product would not produce bright flames.

Adulteration seems to be so much of a problem in India that in 2019 a startup company, Mishry, devoted their efforts exclusively to consumer awareness of food adulteration, which includes hing.

So here we are in the bazaars of India and there is still not much clarity about how asafetida journeyed to the American shores, but my research is ongoing. Any Google search will tell you asafetida has certainly journeyed to our modern-day shores. The ground product, even hing, is readily available on the internet. It seems much of what is for sale comes from India. My perusal of the product reviews indicates the product quality is quite varied and I assume a reflection of the adulteration problems in India. I recommend a certain amount of caution when ordering because even though what I ordered was claimed to be pure asafetida when it arrived the label mentioned it contained "edible gum and wheat".

References

"About Dart." FSSAI. https://fssai.gov.in/dart/. Accessed 7/27/20.

"Asafoetida." *WebMD*. webmd.com/vitamins/ai/ingredientmono-248/asafoetida. Accessed 7/17/20.

Chevallier, Andrew, FNIMH. *Encyclopedia of Herbal Medicine*, 2 ed. Dorling-Kindersley, 2000.

Delaney, Daniel. "What is Asafoetida? / Kale with Chili & Asafoetida Recipe." *Youtube*. www.youtube.com/watch?v=67w296P0SLY February 12, 2011.

Grieve, Maude, FRHS. *A Modern Herbal*. Dorset Press, 1992.

"How to Check Common Spices for Adulterants." *Mishry reviews that matter.* Accessed 7/17/20.

Joshi, Guarang. https://*mishry.com*/a-list-of-common-spices-checking-for-adulterants#test-for-checking-adulteration-in-hing. Accessed 7/17/20.

Iranian Journal of Pharmaceutical Research, 2014 Spring; 13 (2) 523 -530. ncbi.nlm.nih.gov/pmc/articles/PMC4157027/. Accessed 7/17/20.

Pharmacognosy Review, 2012 Jul-Dec; (12): 141-146. National Center for Biotechnology, National Library of Medicine, National Institutes of Health. ncbi.nlm.nih.gov. Accessed 5/12/20.

"Testing Asafoetida (Hing) Adulteration with Foreign Resin." FSSAI. *Youtube*. June 6, 2019. https://www.youtube.com/watch?v=YTrBPL4ID4Y.

"Testing Asafoetida (Hing) Adulteration with Soap or Earthy Matter." FSSAI. *Youtube*. June 18, 2019. https://www.youtube.com/watch?v=THMWjHzVHcI.

Young flat-leaved parsley plants sown directly in container. *Susan Belsinger*

Marge Powell has been an herbalist for over 30 years and an avid plant person her entire life. Her herbal interests span the culinary, the medicinal, and body care aspects as well as growing herbs. She completed a medicinal herbal apprenticeship with Susun Weed and was introduced to herbal body care in workshops by Rosemary Gladstar.

Marge is a passionate cook and most of her cooking is herb-enhanced. She teaches classes in cooking with herbs, making your own medicines, creating lotions and ointments, making soap, and blending scents. She has conducted hands-on workshops on these and other herbal topics across the United States. In 2000 she incorporated Magnolia Hill Soap Co., Inc. (www.magnoliahillsoaps.com) and in 2011 she added Magnolia Hill Nursery which wholesales organic herbs and heirloom vegetables to local garden centers.

She is currently a board member of the International Herb Association (IHA) and the International Herb Association Foundation and is past president of IHA's former Southeastern Region. She has had numerous herbal articles published in IHA's annual Herb of the Year™ publications.

Persil dans un panier (Parsley in a basket). *Alicia Mann*

Eating Parsley

Italian Leaf Parsley Scan. *Stephanie Parello*

An Ode to Parsley

Stephanie Parello

poor parsley gets such a raw deal
relegated to toss-away garnish
yet with such nutrients inside
if only we'd harness

the plant is a beauty
whether flat or curly
a mighty powerhouse
without being surly

now with a hunch to watch out for charlies*
who enjoy chowing parsley for lunch
move them to a vase set well aside
with their own private bunch to munch

and next year—ah next year
parsley's leaves become bitter
with stems oh so tall
no longer a sitter

up high to the heavens
it climbs up to flower
with friends forming a forest
of strong hefty towers

then seeds of the promise
for more garnish next year
if only conditions
are right, true, and clear

which often they are
in my rocky side yard
so for me parsley sows easy
while for others it's hard

finally the roots ready to harvest
perfect for hearty stew or a soup
not bad for some plants that I grew
in a box on my stoop

*caterpillars of black swallowtail butterflies

Black Swallowtail Caterpillar on Parsley. *Public Domain*

While always a scientist at heart, and a baker in practice, **Stephanie Parello** has recently begun to take seriously the art of cooking. Herbs and spices certainly hold a high place in this regard, and learning more about them helps food become medicine—or just that much more enjoyable. Past board member of the Staten Island Herb Society, Stephanie engages in her own herbal studies, the brewing of remedies, and giving talks and presentations in this regard.

Green Sauces:
Parsley Plays a Leading Part

Susan Belsinger

I love condiments and all sorts of sauces—so much so that I have taught classes on cooking with condiments. They add flavor and can embellish just about any food. Since there is an infinite number of green sauces around the globe, and there is some confusion as to the difference between *green sauce, sauce vert, salsa verde, chimichurri, chermoula, pesto* and *pistou*, I decided to define some of these terms as well as share my thoughts on proper terminology. One of the main ingredients that most green sauces have in common is parsley.

I got onto this quest because 1) parsley is the 2021 Herb of the Year™ and is featured in a myriad of green sauces and 2) I find just about everyone calling any sauce made with herbs (as well as a variety of other ingredients) a pesto. Pesto is a classic recipe made with a few certain ingredients—read the discussion below. I prefer to actually call it what it is—though you can call it what you will—just make and use these glorious green sauces on a regular basis.

Green Sauces

Generally, a green sauce is an uncooked sauce featuring herbs and most often served at room temperature or slightly chilled. Under the herbal umbrella of global green sauces there are *sauce verte* (French); *salsa verde* (Italian and Mexican); *Grüne Soße* (German); *chimichurri* (Argentinian); *chermoula* (Moroccan); *pesto* (Italian); *pistou* (French); *chatni or green chutney* (Indian); *green herb and chile dipping sauce* (Thailand); and *Zhoug* (Yemen), to name a few. Even the American invention of Green Goddess Dressing could be considered a green sauce.

Recipes for *greensauce* have been recorded as far back as medieval times in Europe and have been documented throughout history. Most call for a mixture of herbs with sorrel being a prominent selection, along with parsley and garlic, especially in English cookery—and most often are served with meat.

Chimichurri. *Susan Belsinger*

Chimichurri

I am quite fond of this thick, Argentinian condiment, which is found on nearly every table there. It is also very popular in Uruguay, and both countries serve this sauce with grilled meat. It is prepared with parsley, oregano, garlic, onion, olive oil, red wine vinegar, and seasoned with salt and pepper and, more often than not, red pepper flakes. The herbs and vegetables are chopped and then the oil and vinegar are stirred in—it is not a puree—it has lots of texture.

Tangy and pungent, it can be served with any food cooked on the grill from meat, poultry, and fish to vegetables. At my house, it is used as a dipping sauce for tortilla chips, raw or steamed veggies, or spooned on tacos, salads, sandwiches, rice, and grains. Chimichurri can be prepared in advance and refrigerated for 24 hours, if needed.

Makes about 1 cup

1/2 cup olive oil
About 2 tablespoons red wine vinegar
3 or 4 cloves garlic, finely chopped or minced
1/3 cup finely chopped fresh parsley
1/3 cup finely chopped fresh cilantro
About 1 1/2 teaspoons fresh chopped oregano leaves
        or 3/4 teaspoon dried oregano
1 to 3 teaspoons hot red pepper flakes
About 1 teaspoon sea salt
Freshly ground black pepper
1 teaspoon or so, fresh squeezed lime or lemon juice

In a bowl, mix the oil, vinegar, and garlic together with a fork. Add the herbs and 1 teaspoon of chile flakes, season with salt and pepper and stir well. This can be pulsed in a food processor though take care to leave some texture.

Allow to sit for at least 30 minutes for flavors to meld; it can be made a few hours in advance. Add the lime juice, blend well, and taste for seasoning. Adjust with more chiles, citrus, or vinegar and salt and pepper.

Sauce Verte

Literally, this is the French translation for green sauce. In Renaissance times *sauce verte au pain* made with herbs and oil and bread was used to thicken the sauce; a similar rendition is still made today in Italy. Currently, sauce verte more often refers to a green-colored, herb-flavored mayonnaise. Blanched herbs such as parsley, tarragon, watercress, and sometimes spinach are puréed and added to homemade or store-bought mayonnaise usually flavored with lemon juice. I have also seen recipes with fresh chopped herbs added, which would give it a different texture and it would appear as more of a white sauce with green flecks. It usually accompanies seafood or poultry, though it is good with practically any vegetable and is lovely on sandwiches. I especially like it with oven-roasted potatoes and for dipping artichoke leaves.

Salsa Verde, Italian-style

I have been making versions of this rustic sauce since I lived in Italy in the early 70s and I probably have never made it the same way twice. It nearly always has parsley, garlic, olive oil and a little wine vinegar for acidity. Most often, I use a slice of rustic bread to thicken the sauce, which I sprinkle with a little vinegar and water first and let stand for 10 minutes or so. Most European cuisines use their stale bread to add to sauces, soups and salads.

Although parsley is used year-round nowadays, most of the herbs used are seasonal: cress, sorrel, fennel or lovage in the spring; basil, tarragon, dill or nasturtium in the summer; arugula, parsley, autumn-flush of chickweed, and perhaps a bit of oregano or sage in the fall. My favorite salsa verde is made with wild foraged weeds like chickweed, henbit, purple dead nettle, stinging nettle, dandelion leaves and flowers, garlic mustard, mallow, wood or sheep sorrel, a few violet or plantain leaves, and a little wild monarda for pungency. Use what you have in your garden or yard and experiment with seasonal flavors.

Close-up comparison of flat leaf versus curly leaf parsley. *Susan Belsinger*

Salsa Verde, Italian-style

I enjoy this flavorful sauce on just about any vegetable from fresh crudités like radishes and fennel, springtime asparagus, baby beets and carrots, new potatoes and artichokes, to summer and fall grilled eggplant, squash, onions and peppers. It is great on bread, sandwiches, pizza, pasta, or stirred into soup. Capers, onion and sometimes anchovies or a hardboiled egg are traditional additions to Italian-style salsa verde. This sauce goes well with simply prepared meat, chicken, or fish and pasta. Experiment and replace some of the parsley with basil, use tarragon or dill instead of marjoram, or substitute watercress for the arugula (sometimes called rocket). Exact amounts aren't absolute—if you use more herbs or less—just adjust the amount of oil.

Makes about 2 1/2 cups

1 or 2 one-inch thick slices stale country bread, crusts removed
About 3 tablespoons water mixed with 1 tablespoon vinegar
3 large garlic cloves, slivered
Salt
1 cup packed fresh Italian parsley leaves
1 cup packed fresh basil leaves (summer) or arugula (fall and winter)
Generous cup loosely packed fresh spinach, watercress or dandelion leaves,
            or 1/2 cup sorrel leaves, optional
Handful of fresh marjoram or oregano leaves
About 1/2 cup olive oil
1/4 cup minced sweet onion
2 tablespoons white wine or herb vinegar
About 1 tablespoon capers, rinsed and drained, optional
Salt and freshly ground pepper

Soak the bread in a little water (just enough to moisten) for 10 minutes, then squeeze most of the liquid from it. While the bread is soaking, rough chop the herbs. Pound the garlic with the bread in a large mortar and pestle until mashed. Add a large pinch of salt and a handful of the herbs and pound until the herbs are mashed. Continue adding the herbs a handful at a time drizzling in a little oil as you go, pounding them, until all of the herbs have been added.

Or chop the garlic and herbs in a food processor; add the bread and pulse with about half of the oil. Do not overprocess—leave some texture.

Add the rest of the olive oil to the herbs as if making a mayonnaise, drizzling

Salsa Verde. *Susan Belsinger*

in a little at a time, blending or pulsing to incorporate.

Salsa Verde, Mexican-style

Although this version of salsa verde is distinctly unlike the Italian, it is equally as delicious and can be served in as many ways. Since this recipe derives from Mexico, it uses herbs and foods from their sunny climate. It has similar ingredients to traditional tomato salsa, but, because it is a green sauce, tomatillos are used in place of the tomatoes, though not always. Onions, garlic, and green chiles are added ingredients and the sauce can be mild or really hot depending upon the capsicums that are used. Frequently the chiles are roasted, along with the tomatillos, adding a savory, smoky flavor. Cilantro is the herb of choice, used in small to large amounts, and occasionally some *quelites* (lamb's quarters) or Mexican oregano are added. I have seen recipes that add ripe avocado. The salsa can be prepared with a *molcajete y metate* (a mortar and pestle made from volcanic rock) or, nowadays, it is buzzed in the food processor—be sure to leave some texture.

Salsa verde will keep in the fridge for at least 5 days if avocado isn't added. It adds zest to any Mexican or Southwestern dish from tortilla chips and tacos to quesadillas and burritos and is good with grilled vegetables, seafood, chicken, or meat. Brighten up rice by stirring in a few spoonfuls—I like it especially well with corn-on-the-cob—roll your steamed or roasted corn in the salsa verde and then sprinkle it with some grated queso for a south-of-the-border-inspired treat.

Pesto

Here is the Merriam-Webster definition of pesto: "a sauce made especially of fresh basil, garlic, oil, pine nuts, and grated cheese." First known use of pesto: 1937. History and etymology for pesto: Italian, from *pesto*, adjective, pounded, from *pestare*, to pound, from Late Latin *pistare*, frequentative of Latin *pinsere*.

Yes, a pesto can technically be called a salsa verde because it is a green sauce made of herbs; however, all other green sauces or salsa verde should not be called pesto because they are not this unique and traditional recipe. A true pesto has mainly five ingredients: fresh basil, garlic, olive oil, pine nuts, and a hard-grated Italian cheese. The first three ingredients are essential; however, even in Italy the nuts and cheese vary from region to region. If pine nuts are not available, other nuts can be substituted and I have had pesto in Italy made with Pecorino Romano, Parmigiano Reggiano, and Grana Padana—all hard cheeses that are grated.

I have had versions of pesto from Northern Italy that had cream added to the classic five ingredients; in Tuscany I ate pesto with Italian flat-leaved parsley added; and in Southern Italy with sundried tomatoes and lemon zest added. These were all pestos because they had the essential ingredients that define the dish, though with variations.

I first learned to make pesto in a mortar and pestle and usually do so because I enjoy this ceremony of preparation. Occasionally, however, when I am in a hurry, I use the food processor. Pounding in the mortar gives a different texture to the pesto, whereas in the food processor it is a fairly homogenous texture; be sure not to overprocess and leave some texture rather than making a puree. Pesto does not mean paste.

In her article "Rethinking Pesto Means Breaking the Rules", author Karen Baar states, "True pesto is made with a mortar and pestle, is never cooked, and is served at room temperature." She further reflects on using other herbs and the idea of pesto, "Any number of pesto-like sauces can be made using the fresh greens and herbs that are available in farmers' markets and supermarkets. These recipes break all of those rules. The herbs are chopped, minced and ground in food processors and blenders."

In my opinion and in keeping the integrity of the classic recipe, a pesto is made with the traditional five ingredients that define the dish, perhaps with slight variations by adding another ingredient or two, though not substituting other herbs in place of the inimitable basil. Once you do that, you've got a green sauce or salsa verde—it might be *pesto-like*—however, it is not the real thing. This is my personal point of view and I am sticking to it even though my editor noted, "Susan, I admire your stand on this but think you are losing the battle on what the general public thinks of as pesto sauce."

Pesto, Tuscan-Style

For centuries, Italians have made pesto with a mortar and pestle, hence the name pesto from the verb "pestare", which means to pound or grind. Pesto prepared in this manner is by far the best, for it has a wonderful emulsion and is thick and creamy. The flavors are also more intense—the garlic is more pungent, the nuts are sweeter and more resinous, and the basil is rich in perfume. Tuscans often mellow pesto with the bright green taste of parsley.

Nowadays, many of us use the food processor to make pesto since it is quick and easy. Directions for both methods are given below.

Traditionally, pesto is served with pasta; however it is a popular accompaniment to many other foods. I prefer Parmigiano Reggiano for making pesto although other hard Italian cheeses work well. Depending on the time of year and the type of basil and garlic that you use, flavors will vary in strength, so you may have to add more of one or the other. If the pesto tastes sharp, add more cheese; if it is too thick, thin it with a little olive oil.

Although it isn't as wonderful as just-made, leftover pesto is still good after three or four days, if it is kept tightly-covered in the refrigerator. The top layer will darken some; just stir it in. This recipe was first published in <u>Basil: An Herb Lover's Guide</u> by Thomas DeBaggio and Susan Belsinger, Interweave Press, 1996.

Makes about 1 1/2 cup; enough to dress 1 pound of dry pasta
or about 1 1/2 pounds fresh pasta

5 cloves garlic, peeled and sliced
1/4 cup pine nuts
Salt
4 cups packed basil leaves or 3 cups packed basil + 1 cup Italian flat leaf
parsley for Tuscan-style pesto
1/2 cup freshly grated Parmigiano Reggiano or Pecorino Romano cheese
About 3/4 cup extra virgin olive oil

Combine the garlic and pine nuts in a large mortar with a few pinches of salt and crush them with the pestle into a smooth paste. Add the basil to the mortar, a handful at a time, crushing the leaves against the sides with the pestle. With each handful of herb add a small drizzle of olive oil to make the grinding easier. The mixture will be like a coarse, thick paste until all of the oil is added.

Drizzle the remaining olive oil in slowly, a bit at a time, as you work it in. The pesto should become very smooth and there should not be any big pieces. Stir in the cheese. Once most of the oil is added, taste for seasoning and adjust with a little more oil, cheese, or salt.

If you are using a food processor, combine the garlic, pine nuts, basil, a few pinches of salt, and a few tablespoons of the oil. Process until mixed. Add the cheese and most of the remaining oil and process until homogenous; do not completely purée, leave a little texture. Taste for seasoning, and add the rest of the oil, and a little more cheese or salt, if desired.

Green Goodness Dressing

This recipe was originally published in *Gourmet Magazine* in 1980, when Carolyn Dille and I co-authored the year-long series "A Calendar of Herbs." It is a classic—still as delicious and versatile now as it was then—it is our version of a green goddess dressing. It is a gorgeous emerald green color; the tangy, herby dressing goes well with salads—grain, potato, pasta, greens; and just about any crudités, blanched or steamed vegetables. Add any other herbs that you like or have on hand in place of some of the parsley. Most green goddess dressings have mayonnaise added. If you prefer it creamier, use half the amount of olive oil called for and stir in 1/2 cup mayonnaise at the end—if you blend or process it—it will become liquidy rather than thicken the dressing.

Makes about 1 1/2 cups

2 cups packed parsley leaves
Juice of 1 lime or lemon
1 tablespoon white wine vinegar
2 garlic cloves, crushed
1 teaspoon Dijon-style mustard
1/2 teaspoon salt
Freshly ground pepper
1 cup olive oil

Blend all of the ingredients at low speed in a blender for 1 minute, and at high speed for 30 seconds, or until the mixture is bright green. Adjust the seasoning with lemon juice, vinegar, or salt if necessary.

The dressing keeps, covered and chilled, for 1 week. Stir the dressing before using and serve at cool room temperature.

This article is excerpted from Susan's forthcoming book *The Perfect Bite*, due out Spring 2021.

References

Arndt, Alice. *Seasoning Savvy: How to Cook with Herbs, Spices and Other Flavorings*. The Haworth Herbal Press, 1999.

Baar, Karen. "Rethinking Pesto Means Breaking the Rules." *New York Times*. https://www.nytimes.com/1997/10/08/dining/rethinking-pesto-means-breaking-the-rules.html. Accessed 6/5/20.

Belsinger, Susan, and Carolyn Dille. *Herbs in the Kitchen*. Interweave Press, 1992.

Davidson, Alan. *The Penguin Companion to Food*. Penguin Books, 2002.

DeBaggio, Thomas, and Susan Belsinger. *Basil: An Herb Lover's Guide*. Interweave Press, 1996.

Devi, Yamuni. *Lord Krishna's Cuisine: The Art of Indian Vegetarian Cooking*. Bala Books, 1987.

Herbst, Sharon Tyler. *The New Food Lover's Companion*. Barron's Educational Series, Inc., 1995.

"Pesto." *Merriam-Webster*. https://www.merriam-webster.com/dictionary/pesto. Accessed 6/5/20.

Root, Waverly. *The Food of Italy*. Vintage Books, 1977.

See bio page 8.

Parsley bouquet on the windowsill. Treat parsley like a cut flower and it will last over a week. Change the water every few days. *Susan Belsinger*

Let's Party with Parsley!

Gert Coleman

Often called the Herb of Festivity, parsley has always been invited to parties. Originally an effective and dependable medicinal herb, parsley has emerged as a congenial culinary herb, celebrated for increasing the fun, flavor, and safety of social gatherings. Ancient Romans wore parsley chaplets at feasts to induce enjoyment and prevent inebriation; some crafted parsley necklaces to absorb food and drink odors. Parsley was chewed between courses to freshen breath and reduce flatulence. Sprigs were eaten the day after to alleviate hangover and indigestion.

Once believed to be an antidote to food poisoning, cooks added parsley to plates and buffets to ward off contamination. During the reign of Emperor Charlemagne (742-814 AD), sprigs of parsley and vials of dill oil were placed prominently on tables at royal feasts to reduce the noisy discomforts of guests who overindulged.

In many parts of Europe, brides and grooms wore parsley during the wedding rites while singers and dancers adorned themselves with festive wreaths of parsley, rosemary, and myrtle. Spanish brides carried bread and parsley under their arms to repel evil spirits and encourage fertility. Amulets of parsley were tucked under shirts or bodices to attract romance. German lovers once sowed their names with parsley seeds to express fidelity.

Linked to love and lust, parsley has been considered an aphrodisiac, believed "to revitalize tired members" (*Herbal Love Potions* 136). French and German red-light districts were sometimes known as "parsley alleys". According to legend, chewing parsley leaves can stimulate libido and enhance sexuality. For the best results, according to an article in the *New York Times Magazine*, one should visualize the desired partner, saying, "I welcome love. I am open to romance." To make a romantic liaison last, though, superstition suggests to avoid cutting parsley leaves from the stems, lest you cut off the passion.

Parsley symbolizes fertility and prosperity. Folks in rural England once told children they came from the parsley bed. A tall crop of parsley was thought to

Parsley for sale at Rennes Farmers Market, France. *Peter Coleman*

foretell a birth in the family; a verdant crop indicated the matron of the family ruled the household. To some, a strong stand of parsley predicted good health and long life for the gardener. Medieval chefs added parsley as a vegetable to liven up stews, soups, and pottages. Because its nutritional content can act like a multivitamin, many couples reportedly enjoyed renewed vigor in the bedroom, with parsley gaining a reputation for cupidity. Monasteries grew it only for medicinal purposes and, until the 10 century, clergy tried to keep parsley away from the general population by reinforcing its connection to death, the Devil, and the Underworld.

With its high mineral count, parsley can revitalize and energize our bodies and spirits. In the Language of Flowers, parsley represents feasting, festivity, and gratitude. Many savory dishes presented at parties, family gatherings, and celebrations are sprinkled with this bright green herb. And at such meals we are often grateful to see each other, enjoy the family, and create new memories. Though our gatherings have been scaled down due to the coronavirus outbreak, let's invite parsley to our everyday feasts to rediscover what parsley can do to us and for us.

Recipes

Parsley has always been part of my feasts and parties. When I first started cooking, I only used dried parsley, but once I started growing it in my garden, I began to use fresh as often as possible. For the following recipes, use either fresh or dried. The parsley measurements below are only a guide, add more or less as it suits, and always sprinkle a little extra on top.

Parsley Chive Dip for Raw Vegetables

Parley pairs well with garlic and chives, moderating their bite with a fresh green taste. I have made this dip with both fresh and dried parsley, and either way, it's a hit at family events, luncheons for friends, or even as a simple summertime meal. Serve with raw carrots, broccoli, cauliflower, celery, peppers, summer squash, and cherry tomatoes. The more colors, the better!

Serves 4 to 6

1 cup cottage cheese
1/2 cup sour cream
2/3 cup mayonnaise

2 tablespoons chopped parsley, fresh or dried
1 tablespoon chopped fresh chives
2 to 3 cloves garlic, minced
2 tablespoons finely chopped onion
1 teaspoon Worcestershire sauce
1/4 teaspoon Tabasco sauce or your favorite hot sauce
Salt, optional
Pepper

In a mixing bowl, mix cottage cheese, sour cream and mayonnaise until smooth. Stir in the remaining ingredients and chill in refrigerator until ready to serve.

Parsley Lemon Butter

Serve over vegetables, pasta, or filet mignon. Add minced garlic for additional flavor. Excellent for making garlic bread, too.

8 tablespoons butter
3 to 4 tablespoons fresh parsley, chopped
1/2 teaspoon grated lemon zest
Dash crushed red pepper, optional

Place butter in a glass bowl and allow to come to room temperature. Mix in parsley, lemon zest, and crushed red pepper. Keep refrigerated until ready to serve.

Parsley Stuffed Mushrooms

Large mushrooms for stuffing are found in supermarkets around the holidays, usually in 3- to 5-pound boxes. Serve these delicious stuffed mushrooms as an appetizer or a side dish. For extra flavor, crush the dried oregano and thyme between your palms to release the scent. The original recipe calls for "lots of fresh parsley" but you can decide for yourself how much parsley makes this dish. A bunch of store-bought parsley is more than you'll need, but I often chop the whole bunch and leave in a pretty dish on the counter to sprinkle on just about everything for the next few days. It's such a treat to have on hand!

Yields 12 servings

3 pounds large stuffing mushrooms
1/2 cup extra virgin olive oil
1 cup fine dry bread crumbs
1 cup grated Parmesan cheese
3 tablespoons fresh parsley chopped, or 2 tablespoons dried, plus more to
        sprinkle on top
1 teaspoon dried oregano, crushed between your palms
1 teaspoon dried thyme, crushed between your palms
1 to 2 sticks butter
Pepper
Salt, optional

Clean mushrooms with a moist paper towel. Remove the stems and set aside for another use. Preheat oven to 425° F.

In a large bowl, mix together bread crumbs and Parmesan cheese, then add the parsley, oregano, and thyme. Add pepper to taste; salt is optional. Add just enough olive oil to make the mixture manageable for stuffing—just a few drizzles.

Place mushrooms on a large baking sheet and drizzle lightly with oil and salt, if using, before stuffing. To stuff caps, make a neatly packed mound atop each mushroom. Place a nice pat of butter on each one.

Bake at 425° F for about 20 minutes. Serve warm or at room temperature.

References

Arrowsmith, Nancy. *Essential Herbal Wisdom: A Complete Exploration of 50 Remarkable Herbs*. Llewellyn, 2007. 193-208.

Keville, Kathy. Herbs: *An Illustrated Encyclopedia*. Barnes and Noble, 1997. 35-36.

Kowalchik, Claire and William H. Hylton, eds. *Rodale's Illustrated Encyclopedia of Herbs*. Rodale Press, 1987. 407-409.

Lee, William H. and Lynn Lee. *Herbal Love Potions*. Keats Publ. Inc., 1991. 136-137.

Morrison, Dorothy. *Bud, Blossom, & Leaf: The Magical Herb Gardener's Handbook*. Llewellyn, 2001. 162.

Pollux, Amaria. *Wicca Now*. "The Wonderful Magical Properties of Parsley." https://wiccanow.com/magickal-properties-of-parsley/. Accessed 11/2/20.

Romain, Effie and Sue Hawkey. *Herbal Remedies in Pots*. Dorling Kindersley, 1996.

Wollan, Malia. "How to Make a Love Potion." *New York Times Magazine*. 8/30/20.

See bio page 65.

Curly parsley showing blooms. *Susan Belsinger*

Susan Belsinger

Kitchen Tips

Whether it's fresh from your garden or bought from the store, always wash your parsley. Curly parsley especially can hold bits of soil. Shake it dry, let it drain in the drainer, or wrap lightly in a dry kitchen towel to catch excess water.

When chopping fresh parsley, you want it dry. Do not chop the leaves when wet as they can turn into a watery, unappetizing mess.

Rub fresh parsley on cutting boards to clean and to eliminate the lingering odors of garlic and onion.

A Taste for Parsley

Kathleen Connole

Like many of us, all I really knew of parsley as a child was as a garnish on the plate at a nice restaurant that could freshen your breath. I do not remember any of the cooks in our family using it. They might have had dried parsley on the spice shelf, but I do not remember it being used in any way that I could now recognize.

In the 1970s, on my own and learning about vegetarianism, my favorite cookbook was *Diet for a Small Planet* by Frances Moore Lappe, which promoted the concept of complementary proteins as an alternative to a meat-based diet. We still use recipes from this book, and two of our favorites introduced us to parsley. We learned how to make delicious Tabouli, a "Zesty Lebanese Salad", which uses fresh parsley and fresh mint. The following casserole recipe is our adaptation and a great way to use fresh spinach. A nice accompaniment to this meal would be a contrasting, brightly colored vegetable such as carrot, sweet potato, or yellow squash.

Spinach Parsley Casserole

4 to 6 servings

1 cup raw brown rice, cooked
1 cup grated sharp cheddar cheese
2 eggs, beaten
1/2 teaspoon salt
1/2 teaspoon black pepper
1 pound fresh spinach, chopped
1 bunch flat leaf parsley, chopped
2 tablespoons wheat germ (or flaxseed meal)
1 tablespoon extra virgin olive oil

In a large bowl, combine cooked rice and cheese. In a separate bowl, combine eggs, salt, and pepper. Add these two mixtures together, then stir in the spinach and parsley. Pour into an oiled casserole dish. Combine the wheat germ or flaxseed meal with the olive oil and spread over the top of the casserole.

Bake in a 350° F oven for 35 minutes or until top is golden brown.

Pounds of Parsley. *Karen England*

See bio page 54.

Parsley:
Well-Used, Well-Deserved,
and Well-Preserved

Pat Crocker

For thousands of years parsley has been nourishing man as well as horses.
-Sylvia Windle Humphrey, A Matter of Taste

It may come as a surprise to learn that the ubiquitous herb we call parsley was the favourite pasture cover of the Greek gods, who raised their immortal, fire-breathing steeds on it. Perhaps not too astonishing if we consider that it was thought to have sprung from the blood of the Greek hero, Archemorus. One wonders if possibly the moon creature itself, Arion, foal of Gaia (the Earth), nibbled on the green garnish between stints as the chosen horse of Adrastus, king of Argos.

And while pondering the diet of fabled horses, one might also consider that English men and women alive and presumably thriving at the time of Queen Elizabeth consumed a dish of Parsley Pie. Well, why not? Good enough for mythological horses, good enough for mere mortals.

Here's a recipe for Parsley Pie from an 1863 book that Maude Grieve cites in *Culinary Herbs and Condiments: Lay a fowl or a few bones of the scrag of veal seasoned, into a dish: scald a colander-full of picked parsley in milk; season, and add it to the fowl or meat, with a teacupful of any sort of good broth, or weak gravy. When it is baked, pour it into a quarter of a pint of cream, scalded, with the size of a walnut of butter, and a little flour. Shake it round to mix with the gravy already in. Lettuces, white mustard leaves, or spinach, may be added to the Parsley, and scalded before being put in.*

Indeed, as Sylvia Humphrey advised in 1965, parsley is a powerhouse of nutrients. One half pound of this deep green herb delivers 439 mg of calcium (recommended RDI is 1,000; milk has about 300 mg in 1 cup), 190 mg of phosphorus (1 chicken thigh, 150 mg); 10 mg of iron (1 cup spinach, .81 mg);

37.36 IU Vitamin A (17,000 in 1/2 cup cooked carrot); and 438 mg Vitamin C (an orange delivers 53.2 mg). Not bad for that often sad-looking, wilted sprig languishing on the plates of contemporary diners.

For the ancients, parsley was a symbol of victory, joy, even revelry and festivity. Since he was thought to have the power of speech, did Arion kick up his heels, toss his glossy mane, and whinny, "Man, I'm feeling my parsley!"'?

Parsley as a Significant Ingredient

Over time, the custom of using herbs in great handfuls, quantities large enough to be truly nourishing has been, for the most part, lost. However, I would argue that because it is so commonly available and at the same time uniquely beneficial, what better herb to reawaken that tradition than parsley?

The variety of parsley known as Hamburg is grown for its enlarged and fleshy taproot. In his *Gardeners' Dictionary* in 1771, Philip Miller writes, "the large-rooted Parsley…under cultivation develops both a parsnip-like, as well as a turnip-shaped form…the roots being six times as large as the common Parsley." Miller goes on to describe the "long white" and the "round sugar" forms as being commonly sold in London markets at that time.

If you can find it at a farmers' market—if not, you can easily grow it—I recommend that you scrub and trim an equal number of carrots, parsnips, and Hamburg parsley roots. Drizzle with olive oil and toss together with a handful of chopped fresh parsley, salt, and pepper. You can add a dash of nutmeg or cinnamon but the sweetness of the parsnips is all you really need. Sauté all together in melted butter over medium-high heat for about 12 minutes or until crisp-tender. Delicious.

Maude Grieve advises that the "Neapolitan, or celery-leaved Parsley, is grown for the use of its leaf-stalks, which are blanched and eaten like those of celery." This inspired me to try making a simple salad of equal parts celery sticks (about 1/4-inch thick and 1 to 2 inches long), parsnip sticks, carrot sticks, and Neapolitan parsley stalks, cut to the same length. Sauté all together in a generous glug of olive oil over medium-high heat for about 12 minutes or until crisp-tender. Serve over a nest of baby arugula and drizzle with freshly squeezed lemon juice. Divine.

Hamburg Parsley. *Deb Jolly*

Recipes

We all know and love Tabbouleh with its bulgur wheat, chopped fresh mint, and parsley, sometimes tossed with summer-ripened chunks of tomatoes and dressed with lemon juice and cold-pressed olive oil. But what other dishes can benefit from generous amounts of the lightly spiced, anise- and lemon-tasting fresh parsley? Try experimenting by adding more-than-usual amounts to sauces, salads, side dishes, and main course favourites.

Grieve warns us, though, to never chop parsley destined for a sauce. Instead, she tells us to pick, remove the stalks, and blanch whole leaves for 1 minute in boiling water with 1/2 teaspoon baking soda and a pinch of salt. Lift out of the water and pat dry. Sauté in butter that you would use in the sauce and "it will break into tiny shreds, and both odour and flavour are better than if chopped in the usual way."

The following parsley-friendly recipes will get you started thinking of this herb as a bona fide ingredient instead of the timid seasoning it has become. Don't be parsimonious with the parsley!

Parsleyed Nut Loaf

Makes 2 to 4 servings

3 tablespoons olive oil
1 medium onion, chopped
1/2 red pepper, chopped
12 mushrooms, sliced
1 cup chopped fresh parsley
1 cup chopped salted cashew nuts
1/2 cup bread crumbs
1/4 cup chopped chives
2 tablespoons chopped fresh basil
1 large egg, lightly beaten
1/2 teaspoon sea salt

Preheat oven to 350° F. Line the bottom and 2 long sides of a loaf pan with parchment paper.

Heat oil in a large skillet over medium-high heat. Sauté onion, pepper, and mushrooms for 12 minutes or until onion is transparent and peppers are tender. Transfer to a large mixing bowl.

Add parsley, nuts, bread crumbs, chives, and basil and stir to combine. Toss egg and salt into the mixture. Spoon into prepared loaf pan, pressing on the mixture with the back of the spoon. Bake in preheated oven for 30 to 40 minutes or until the top is browned and the sides have begun to pull away from the pan.

Parsley and Rice Stuffed Peppers

Makes 4 servings

4 large green, red, or yellow bell peppers (poblanos also work)
3 tablespoons olive oil
1 small onion, chopped
2 cloves garlic, finely chopped
1 cup cooked brown or white rice
3 cups chopped fresh parsley

Preheat oven to 350° F. Line a rimmed baking sheet with parchment paper.

Bring a large pot of water to a boil over high heat. Slice the stem end off the peppers, discard, and remove the fleshy ribs and seeds. Lower whole peppers into the boiling water and cook for 6 minutes or until crisp-tender. Remove using tongs and set, cut side down, onto a cooling rack to drain.

Heat olive oil in a large skillet over medium-high heat. Stir in onion and cook, stirring frequently for 7 minutes or until soft. Stir in garlic and cook, stirring frequently for 3 minutes. Add rice and parsley and stir well to combine. Taste and add salt as desired.

Spoon filling into peppers and arrange on prepared baking sheet. Cover with foil and bake for 30 minutes. Remove foil and return to oven to bake for 10 minutes or until peppers are tender.

Green Cabbage with Tomato Sauce

I use chopped cabbage in a lot of recipes. You could also simmer the cabbage whole then cut it into wedges, and spoon the sauce over but that takes longer to cook the cabbage.

Makes 4 servings

1 small to medium head green cabbage
3 tablespoons olive oil
1 small onion, chopped
1/2 green pepper, chopped
3 cloves garlic, finely chopped
1 cup chopped parsley
1 28-ounce can diced tomatoes with juice
1 tablespoon freshly squeezed lemon juice
Sea salt to taste

Wash, core, and shred the cabbage. Transfer to a large pot and cover with water. Cover and bring to a boil over high heat. Reduce heat and simmer for 10 minutes or until crisp tender. Set a colander in the sink and pour cabbage into it. Allow to drain while you prepare the tomato sauce.

Heat oil in a skillet over medium-high heat. Stir in onion and pepper and cook, stirring frequently for 7 minutes or until soft and fragrant. Stir in garlic and parsley and cook for 3 minutes. Add tomatoes and lemon juice. Bring to a simmer and cook, stirring frequently for 5 minutes. Taste and add salt as desired.

Edible landscaping: green cabbages amid the parsley. *Pat Kenny*

Parsley Jelly

–from *Preserving* (HarperCollins) by Pat Crocker

Makes 7 8-ounce jars

2 cups lightly packed, coarsely chopped fresh parsley
3 cups boiling water
1+ cups unsweetened apple juice
2 tablespoons cider vinegar or white wine vinegar
2 tablespoons freshly squeezed lemon juice
4 1/2 cups granulated sugar
1 packet (1-3/4 ounces) pectin crystals
1/4 cup finely chopped hot chile pepper or to taste, optional

Place parsley in a non-reactive teapot or bowl with a tight-fitting lid. Pour boiling water over parsley and cover with lid. Let stand until cool. This takes an hour or longer.

Heat 7 1-cup capacity jars in a canning pot in boiling water and scald the lids, lifter, funnel, and tongs.

Strain off the parsley infusion into a 4-cup liquid measuring cup. Discard the herbs. Add enough apple juice to bring the total liquid to 4 cups. Pour parsley/apple liquid into a canning kettle. Add vinegar and lemon juice. Increase heat and bring to a boil over medium heat, stirring constantly.

Add sugar, one cup at a time, stirring after each addition. Bring to a full rolling boil. Add pectin and boil for 1 minute. Remove from heat. Skim and discard any foam. If using chile pepper, let jelly sit for up to 30 minutes before adding chile to the jelly.

Fill hot jars, leaving a 1/4-inch headspace. Run a thin nonmetallic utensil around the inside of the jar to allow air to escape. Add more hot jelly if necessary, to leave a 1/4-inch headspace. Wipe rims, top with flat lids, and screw on metal rings. Return jars to the hot water bath, topping the canner up with hot water if necessary. Bring to a full rolling boil and process jars for 10 minutes.

Remove canner lid and wait 5 minutes before removing jars to a towel or rack to cool completely. Check seals, label and store in a cool place for up to 1 year.

References

Crocker, Pat. *Preserving*. HarperCollins, 2011.

Grieve, Maude. *Culinary Herbs and Condiments*. New York: Dover Press Inc, 1971, a reprint of the 1934 Harcourt, Brace + Co. publication.

Humphrey, Sylvia Windle. *A Matter of Taste: The Definitive Seasoning Cookbook*. New York: Macmillan Co., 1965.

Pat Crocker's mission in life is to write with insight and experience, cook with playful abandon, and eat parsley with gusto. Author of 22 cookbooks, Crocker holds a degree in Food, Nutrition, Consumer, and Family Studies (Ryerson University, Toronto) and is a culinary herbalist with more than 1.25 million books in print and several translated into over 11 languages. She was honored three times by the International Herb Association and also received the 2009 Gertrude H. Foster award from the Herb Society of America for Excellence in Herbal Literature. Her books, *The Juicing Bible and The Vegan Cook's Bible* (both published by Robert Rose), have won "Best in the World" awards from the International Gourmand Culinary Guild.

Read all about parsley and over forty other herbs in Pat's latest book, *The Herbalist's Kitchen* (Sterling Epicure), now available in bookstores everywhere and on her website, www.patcrocker.com.

Star of the Herb Show: Parsley, No Longer Just Garnish!

Karen England

Available fresh year-round in grocery stores practically the world over, parsley, is still incredibly overlooked and underused. Even the acclaimed American chef and food writer James Beard treated parsley as an afterthought. When listing his six favorite herbs in *Beard on Food* (1974), he asserted, "If I had to pick six herbs I couldn't cook without, I'd settle for basil, bay leaf, rosemary, savory, tarragon, and thyme. Parsley too, of course, but that is so universal it goes without saying."

Without saying—until now, that is!

With this Herb of the Year™ book, the International Herb Association is saying what James Beard only hinted at, that parsley is much more than just a sprig on plate.

As a child in the 60s I can remember going out to eat at restaurants for special family occasions, where, at the end of the meal, off to the side of everyone's plates, sat a forlorn sprig of curly parsley and nothing else. My grandmother said that the parsley was a garnish, something to make the plate look appetizing. She also told me that parsley was good for digestion and freshening breath and should be eaten after the meal. Then, demonstrating, she ate her parsley sprig and so did I. Although no one else at the table ate their parsley sprigs, I have eaten the parsley garnish after finishing my plate ever since and, over the years, people who eat out with me often, automatically pass their parsley sprigs to me knowing that I will eat them all, even if they wouldn't.

The practice of using parsley as a garnish has a history that can be traced back to the civilizations of the ancient Romans and Greeks. But so much more than a garnish, parsley can be the main attraction, the true star of the dish and of even the meal, as the following delicious parsley-centric recipes prove.

Cocktail and Appetizer

In the 2009 IHA Herb of the Year™ book about Bay (*Laurus nobilis*), Nancy Momsen gave a recipe for a Bay Martini made with vodka that I have made repeatedly over the last 12 years; it is so very good. In the last few years I have learned a lot more about cocktails generally, and martinis specifically, and one thing I've learned is that, the Bay Martini notwithstanding, I prefer a dry martini made with gin. With that great bay drink as inspiration, I devised a Parsley Martini with Gin and Parsleyed Olives on the side that is, if I do say so myself, divine.

Parsley Martini. *Karen England*

Parsley Martini

Martinis are many times served with olives in them but serve this drink with the following herbed olives on the side as an appetizer. This recipe calls for some prep work but it is sooo worth it!

Makes two very large drinks

8 ounces gin (preferably, Junipero Gin or other juniper-forward gin)
3 ounces very dry vermouth
1/2 fresh bunch of flat leaf parsley, stems and leaves, divided
Pinch of coarse salt, optional
1/2 to 1 teaspoon lemon or lime zest

Starting early on the day that you are going to serve the martinis, combine the parsley stems with the gin and vermouth in a mason jar to macerate, refrigerated, until you are ready to make the cocktails later in the day. (If you macerate the parsley stems in the alcohol for longer than a day, the infusion loses its bright fresh parsley flavor but is still good.) Now is also a good time to put two martini glasses in the freezer to chill for later.

When ready to make and serve the drinks, put the parsley leaves, a pinch of salt, and some lemon or lime zest in the bottom of a cocktail shaker and muddle them to a pulp. Strain the alcohol from the parsley stems into the shaker with the pulp, add lots of ice and stir until very chilled. Strain into two frosty martini glasses and garnish with an, oh so, appropriate parsley sprig.

Parsleyed Olives

Kalamata olives with the pits, drained
A few glugs of fruity olive oil
Some fresh lemon zest and juice
Sliced shallots
Lots of fresh parsley, chopped
Coarse sea salt to taste
Fresh bread, optional

An hour or more before serving, dress the olives in the rest of the ingredients except the bread and chill. Serve the olives alongside the martinis, add some optional fresh bread to sop up the olive marinade and don't forget to provide a small plate for stashing the spent olive pits.

Parsleyed Olives. *Karen England*

Pierre Franey's *Persil a la Creme*
(Lightly-Creamed Parsley Served as a Vegetable)

Pierre Franey, best known for the long running New York Times quick cooking column "60-Minute Gourmet" and his 20-year collaboration with Craig Claiborne, wrote that his Creamed Parsley recipe was what "most Americans would consider a highly unusual vegetable dish". Understatement. This simple dish is so special that, for me, it beats out creamed spinach for an honored place at the Thanksgiving table. If you use creamed spinach as an ingredient in other dishes such as lasagna as cookbook author Cristina Ferrare does, or on the steakhouse favorite, Creamed Spinach Burgers, as many chefs do, consider using this creamed parsley instead! Note: This recipe can be prepared ahead of time and reheated gently in a double boiler before serving. Also, it freezes well, so you can have it anytime.

Serves the Roman legions....

2 1/2 pounds fresh parsley (about 14 bunches of parsley! Yes, you read that
   correctly!)
4 tablespoons butter
1 shallot, minced
1/2 to 1 pint heavy cream
Salt and freshly ground pepper to taste

Rinse the parsley well in cold water and drain. Cut off and discard the stems so you only have leaves left. Heat a large pot of water to boiling and add the parsley and cook for 3 to 5 minutes. Immediately remove the parsley and plunge it into an ice bath to stop the cooking. Drain the parsley and squeeze out the moisture. Chop the cooked parsley finely with a knife.

In a large sauté pan, melt the butter and sauté the shallot until tender. Add the chopped cooked parsley, stirring well, and cook together until most of the moisture is cooked away. Stir in the cream and heat through, mixing well. Season with salt and pepper and serve warm.

Crocked Turkey Cider Stew with Parsley Dumplings

This dish started out life in my family as a fairly straightforward, old-fashioned British beef-and-cider stew recipe with parsley dumplings but has morphed over the last 40 years into a turkey cider stew, still with parsley dumplings, but made in the crock pot. Dumplings were, according to the Reader's Digest Association of London, England, invented in Norfolk in the 16th century and are "... one of the bastions of English national cuisine.... Parsley seasoning is Devon's contribution to the dumpling galaxy; few better companions could be found to set off a cider-flavoured stew." Hard cider is sold like wine, draft cider is sold like beer, and plain cider is sold like juice. They all make for a fine stew.

Makes 10 to 12 servings

3 to 4 tablespoons well-seasoned flour*, or plain flour
3- to 4-pound turkey breast or thighs, skin on, bone in
3 tablespoons or more olive oil
10 ounces cider
20 ounces rich chicken or turkey stock
4 carrots, chopped into 1/4-inch chunks
3 ribs celery, chopped into 1/4-inch chunks
2 yellow onions, chopped into 1/4-inch chunks
1 large turnip, chopped into 1/4-inch chunks
1 to 2 fresh or dried bay leaves

*To make well-seasoned flour, combine 3 to 4 tablespoons all-purpose flour, 1 teaspoon coarse sea salt, 1 teaspoon freshly ground black pepper or seasoned pepper, and 1 teaspoon sugar.

Remove the turkey skin and cut the meat off the bone, into 2- to 3-inch chunks (reserve the skin and bones for making stock another day). Coat the meat chunks with well-seasoned flour and, in a large sauté pan, cook the coated meat in olive oil until browned, then put into a crockpot. ("Roux" any remaining flour, if there is any, from coating the turkey meat by cooking it in the oil left in the sauté pan.) Deglaze the pan with the cider, then add the stock, and simmer briefly to thicken.

Meanwhile put the vegetable chunks and bay leaves into the crockpot on top of the browned turkey meat. Pour in the cider and stock deglazing liquid. Cover the crockpot with the lid and cook on HIGH for 4 to 5 hours (or on LOW for longer).

After 4 or 5 hours (or more depending on which setting you used, HIGH or LOW), when the stew is cooked, put in the dumplings, recipe follows, replace the lid, and cook on LOW until ready to eat (20 minutes minimum).

Dumpling Recipe

2 1/2 cups all-purpose flour
1 teaspoon coarse salt
1 tablespoon baking powder
1/2 to 1 tablespoon sugar
3 tablespoons fresh parsley, finely chopped
Fine zest of 1 lemon
4 tablespoons olive oil
1 cup milk

Mix together the dry ingredients with the parsley and lemon zest. Add oil and mix until crumbly. Add the milk, stirring just until moistened and drop by spoonfuls onto the stew in the crockpot. Cover and cook on LOW 20 minutes or so.

Tabbouleh

You may make the popular deli salad, rich with parsley, called tabbouleh, which, according to Martha Rose Shulman, "... we think of as a bulgur salad with lots of parsley and mint. But real Lebanese tabbouleh is a lemony herb salad with a little bit of fine bulgur, an edible garden that you can scoop up with romaine lettuce heart leaves or simply eat with a fork." I strongly recommend following Ina Garten's Chicken with Tabbouleh method with your recipe of choice: "Tabbouleh was always popular at the Barefoot Contessa but I wanted to make it into a main course. I added diced roasted chicken and it was an immediate hit. Serve it as a first course for a summer dinner, for lunch in pita bread, or pack it in containers for a picnic at the beach."

References

Franey, Pierre. "60-Minute Gourmet." *New York Times*, Sept. 14, 1983.

Garten, Ina. *Barefoot Contessa Family Style*. Clarkson Potter, 2002.

Farmhouse Cookery. The Reader's Digest Association Limited, London, 1980.

"James Beard's Six Essential Herbs." *James Beard Foundation*. Blog 1/24/17. https://www.jamesbeard.org/blog/james-beards-six-essential-herbs. Accessed 11/16/20.

Momsen, Nancy. "Bay Martini." International Herb Association. *Bay (Laurus nobilis) Herb of the Year 2009*. 73.

"Parsley: a Popular Herb with a Long History." *Redlands Daily Facts*. https://www.redlandsdailyfacts.com/2015/11/23/parsley-a-popular-herb-with-a-long-history/. Accessed 11/16/20.

"Pleasing the Palate of James Beard." *Columbia Daily Tribune*, 6/8/15. https://www.columbiatribune.com/article/20150609/Lifestyle/306099915. Accessed 11/16/20.

Shulman, Martha Rose. "A Focus on Fresh Herbs." *New York Times*, 6/15/09. https://www.nytimes.com/2009/06/15/health/nutrition/15recipehealth.html. Accessed 11/16/20.

Simonson, Robert. *The Martini Cocktail*. Ten Speed Press, 2019.

Whitaker, Jan. "Why the Parsley Garnish?" *Restaurant-ing Through History*, 3/22/15. https://restaurant-ingthroughhistory.com/2015/03/22/why-the-parsley-garnish-2/. Accessed 11/16/20.

Karen England is the president of and newsletter editor-in-chief for the San Diego Horticultural Society. She is a blogger, https://edgehillherbfarm.blog/, Instagram influencer, @edgehillherbfarm, and herbal entrepreneur. She gardens and lives on two acres in beautiful Vista, California. She can be reached at k-england@cox.net.

Positively Parsley

Donna Frawley

Parsley is the first herb I remember. My mom only grew three herbs—curly parsley, dill, and chives. She would harvest the leaves, bring them inside, and snip to serve on top of buttered new potatoes or roll her famous salmon ball in a mixture of snipped parsley and walnuts. I remember seeing parsley as a plate decoration in restaurants, but later realized it was so much more than that.

Parsley has three common varieties: flat leaf or Italian, curly leaf, and parsnip-rooted (Hamburg). I grow Italian and curly parsley every year. In Michigan, parsley may winter over, depending on the weather, but I treat it as an annual and buy new plants every spring. If I get some volunteer seedlings from last year's plants, I consider it a blessing and am happy to use them in my cooking or sell to a local market.

Parsley is classified as a biennial, which means the leaves grow the first year and it flowers and makes seeds the second year. However, because of our short growing season, the grower needs to start the seeds so early for them to look good when we are buying them, that sometimes in August they begin to send up stiff stalks with flowers. I just keep cutting the flower stem off to help the plant continue to produce leaves. Toward the end of the summer I let some stalks go to flower and make seeds which may make new seedlings in the spring, but I don't count on it. If you are starting your own seeds, it is best to mix the seed with sand and add water to soak them for at least 24 to 72 hours before sowing the seeds. The seeds may take up to 6 weeks to germinate, so be patient.

When harvesting parsley, you want to cut the outside leaves first. If you cut from the inside, you will stunt the plant since the new growth comes from the center. If you do not harvest the outermost leaves, they will eventually turn brown and need to be cut off and thrown away or composted. By harvesting from the outside, you increase your overall harvest and improve the continued growth and appearance of the plant all season. After you cut your parsley, use

Close-up detail of curly and flat parsley leaves. *Susan Belsinger*

it fresh or store in a moist paper towel that is put into a zippered bag, then the refrigerator. During the growing season you can also chop it up and put it in a storage container in the refrigerator so it is convenient to use fresh for any number of dishes.

To preserve parsley for later, dry it in a dehydrator or freeze it. You can easily snip fresh leaves into a small airtight container and put into the freezer. Another way is to snip leaves into an ice cube tray, add a little water, then freeze until solid. Crack out the frozen cubes and store in the freezer in a zippered bag. Be sure to date and label your bag or container so you know what it is and when you put it in the freezer. The little bit of water with frozen herb cubes won't be a problem when adding to a simmering pot of tomato sauce or soup, but for other dishes, use the frozen parsley you snipped into a container.

Parsley can be used fresh in salads or cooked in soups and stews. Add the leaves to your simmering pot during the last half hour of cooking. Italian parsley is more flavorful and tender than the curly parsley, but the curly is easier to snip. Both are rich in vitamins A and C and iron. Parsley is one of the main ingredients in Bouquet Garni along with thyme and bay leaf, a great blend for soups and stews. I use dried parsley in many of the 60 culinary mixes that I package: *Dill Dip for Vegetables, Herb Lemon Butter for Chicken or Fish, Herbed Rice, Holiday Rice, Italian Dressing Mix, Spaghetti Sauce Herbs, Super Seasoning, Scampi Seasoning, Chicken Soup, Cream of Broccoli Soup, Bouquet Garni, Salad Herbs*. I use fresh parsley in my *Italian Vinegar*.

At home, I use fresh or dried in meatballs, meatloaf, many different salads, new potatoes, and home-canned spaghetti sauce, just to name a few.

So, you can see that parsley is quite versatile. Following are some great recipes using parsley.

Salmon Ball with Parsley

This is my mom's recipe, a favorite for decades and requested for every family gathering.

Serves 6 to 8

1 14-ounce can (red or pink) salmon, drained
1 8-ounce package of cream cheese
1 teaspoon grated onion
4 drops liquid smoke
3/4 cup chopped walnuts
Chopped fresh parsley to cover

In a bowl, place salmon, cream cheese, grated onion, and liquid smoke. Mash until well blended. Place walnuts and parsley on waxed paper, mix together then form salmon mixture into a ball and roll in the walnut-parsley mixture. Serve on a platter surrounded by an assortment of crackers.

Quinoa Salad

This perfect summer salad is from my friend Jackie Prevost. Hearty enough for a meal or as a side dish.

Serves 6 to 8

1 cup quinoa, cooked and cooled
1 14-ounce can garbanzo beans, drained
1 cup tomatoes, sliced
1 cup cucumbers, diced
1/2 cup green onions, sliced
2 cloves garlic, finely minced
1/4 cup fresh parsley, chopped
2 tablespoons fresh basil or mint, chopped
1/4 cup extra virgin olive oil
1/4 cup lemon juice, fresh squeezed
1/4 teaspoon pepper

1 teaspoon sea salt
Fresh mint to garnish

Combine all ingredients in a large bowl and gently mix. Cover and refrigerate until ready to serve.

Steak Diane

Sometimes I just make this up to put on grilled steaks.

Serves 8

1/4 cup butter
1/2 cup thinly sliced fresh mushrooms
2 tablespoons minced onion
1 clove garlic, crushed
1/4 teaspoon salt
1 teaspoon lemon juice
1 teaspoon Worcestershire sauce
2 tablespoons snipped fresh parsley
2 tablespoons butter
1 pound beef tenderloin, cut into 8 slices

Melt butter in a medium-sized skillet over medium-high heat. Add mushrooms, onion, garlic, salt, lemon juice, and Worcestershire sauce and stir until the mushrooms are tender. Stir in parsley; keep sauce warm.

Melt 2 tablespoons butter in another skillet. Sauté tenderloin slices over medium-high heat to medium doneness, about 3 to 4 minutes on each side. Turn once. Serve with mushroom-butter sauce on the side or on top of the tenderloin.

Parsley Parmigiano-Reggiano Dressing

This is a great dressing on an antipasto salad which may include different salamis, cheeses, artichoke hearts, tomatoes, peppers, olives, and/or pickled vegetables.

1/2 cup packed fresh flat leaf parsley, rinsed and dried
1/2 cup extra virgin olive oil
1/3 cup Parmigiano-Reggiano cheese, freshly grated
3 tablespoons red wine vinegar
2 teaspoons Dijon mustard
Salt and pepper to taste

Combine the parsley, oil, cheese, vinegar, and mustard in a blender or food processor; blend until the dressing is smooth. Add salt and pepper to taste and set aside until the salad is ready. Refrigerate leftovers.

Fillet of Sole with Parsley

Serves 8

2 eggs
1/2 teaspoon salt
8 sprigs Italian parsley, stripped from stems and finely chopped
4 tablespoons unsalted butter
2 pounds sole fillets
1 cup flour
Additional parsley sprigs, for garnish
Lemon wedges, for garnish

Beat the eggs with the salt in a flat-bottomed bowl until smooth. Stir the parsley into the egg mixture. Melt butter over low heat in a frying pan large enough to hold the fish in one layer. Dredge the sole in the flour, shaking off the excess. Leave the fillets on a lightly floured surface and adjust the heat under the skillet to medium.

Dip the sole fillets into the egg and parsley mixture, covering both sides, then place them in the frying pan and sauté 2 minutes or until pale golden brown on one side. Turn the fillets and cook for 2 more minutes. Serve on a heated platter garnished with parsley sprigs and lemon wedges.

Up close and personal: curly and flat-leaved parsley. *Susan Belsinger*

Donna Frawley started her business in 1983 by selling at her local farmers' market. Having majored in Home Economics and worked at a private country club, she used those skills to develop 60 culinary herb blends, 8 herb-flavored vinegars, and 8 herbal teas. She carries bulk culinary herbs and spices plus fresh herbs that are sold at LaLonde's Market and Eastman Party Store in Midland, Michigan. You can purchase her culinary mixes on her website, www.frawleysfineherbary.com

She has written three books, *The Herbal Breads Cookbook*, *Our Favorite Recipes*, and *Edible Flowers Book*. In addition, she created the DVD *Cooking With Herbs*, and writes a monthly herb column in her local newspaper. In March 2010 she had her first magazine article published in *Herb Companion Magazine*. She also writes a weekly e-newsletter. Donna hosts cooking parties, teaches cooking classes, and speaks on many culinary herb topics. She was a regular instructor at Whiting Forest in Midland, Michigan. Donna's historical fiction novel *Weymouth Place*, set in Dubuque, Iowa, from 1860 to 1875, is due out in the near future.

Grow flat leaf Italian parsley in the vegetable garden and mulch it with wheat straw. *Susan Belsinger*

Parsley as Key Ingredient

Stephen J. Lee, the HerbMeister

Sprinkle with finely chopped fresh parsley, garnish with a big sprig of fresh parsley, surround with small bouquets of freshly harvested garden parsley. Yes, we have all seen thousands of recipes over the years that employ the herb parsley solely for its culinary beautification capabilities rather than for the unique wonder of itself as ingredient.

In this writing I will be exploring and detailing how to use the herb parsley as the main component of a delicious culinary offering rather than just to complement, enhance, or beautify.

If you are from the school that thinks parsley is only good for use as a garnish, think again, and remember as we go along that parsley is a great digestive aid, a natural breath freshener, and an anti-carcinogen. It contains three times the amount of vitamin C as oranges and twice as much iron as spinach. And, especially, know that it bears its own unique, distinct, and special flavor.

As with any specific recipe ingredient, you will want to search out the freshest and best example readily available. There are many types and varieties of parsley—the well-known and ubiquitous Curly, the lesser known Root Hamburg, the slightly bitter Japanese, and, my parsley of choice, the Flat Leaf.

Flat leaf parsley is an herb/vegetable plant that grows somewhat tall, reaching mature heights of 24+ inches. It is traditionally appreciated for its culinary qualities, and is generally considered the more tasty variety. Flat leaf parsley has several varieties including one called Italian Flat Leaf, which tastes slightly peppery and looks a bit like cilantro—a plant that is often called Chinese Parsley—but, while a member of the same family, offers a totally different herb experience.

I remember parsley—the curly variety—in my Grandmother's herb garden since early childhood days. To a descendent of English settlers, it was a necessary component for much of her culinary genius and an important part of the flavor profile of my culinary memory.

In the beginning of the fresh herb awakening of North America in the early 1980s, I discovered the Italian Flat Leaf variety and have been a staunch proponent of its use since those days. I encourage you to find, grow, and use this variety to enhance all of your cooking from this point forward.

I have found that typically a recipe for most every filled-pasta dish calls for a tablespoon or two of finely chopped parsley—assuming that the dish creator is thinking it adds interest, color and maybe, a tad of flavor. However, if one is to truly experience the essence of parsley, then copious quantities of the herb/vegetable must be employed and additional ingredients kept to a minimum as in this recipe I developed for a somewhat elegant, lighter, tasty, and very colorful offering.

Parsley Lasagna

Special note: you need to use very well drained ricotta; it should not seem wet when you poke it with a finger. Most farmers market ricotta meets this criterion; standard supermarket ricotta must be drained in a layer of cheesecloth or a thin kitchen towel sitting in a strainer, lightly weighted, for a good 14+ hours in the refrigerator.

This lasagna is a breeze if you have access to ready-made, refrigerated pasta sheets. If not, with just a little more effort, you can use boxed lasagna noodles. Simply bring a large pot of water to the boil, lightly salt then add the noodles. Cook just until they are al dente, remove, allow to drain, then quickly lay them out on a lightly greased surface to prevent them from sticking together and pat dry with paper towels. Use as you would the sheets in this recipe.

Serves 4

Filling

1 1/2 cups ricotta cheese—see note above
1 tablespoon heavy cream
1 egg yolk
1 large bunch Italian flat leaf parsley, rinsed, drained, thickest stems removed
1/2 cup Parmesan cheese, freshly grated

1 teaspoon kosher salt
1/2 teaspoon black pepper, freshly ground
Zest of 1/2 lemon

Lasagna

8 refrigerated lasagna sheets—see note above
2 cups, very simple tomato sauce—your favorite canned variety
4 ounces, mozzarella cheese, very thinly sliced
1/2 cup Parmesan cheese, freshly shredded, small

Place the ricotta in the work bowl of a food processor fitted with the metal chopping blade. Pulse a few times, then run the machine until the ricotta starts to grow smooth, scraping down the bowl as needed. Add the cream and the egg yolk, pulsing to incorporate into a smooth mixture.

Add the parsley to the food processor—it will probably fill the work bowl. Pulse and scrape until the parsley breaks down enough to combine with the ricotta; run the machine until the mixture is an even green puree with tiny flecks of parsley. Add the Parmesan cheese, salt, black pepper, and lemon zest and process to a smooth combination. Remove from the processor into a bowl and set aside.

Well grease a 6 x 8 inch loaf pan and set aside. Place a large skillet filled with an inch of water over medium heat and bring to a simmer. Cut the prepared lasagna sheets into 6 x 8 inch triangles that will lay flat in the loaf pan, reserving any remaining portions of the lasagna sheets for another use—like cutting into noodles and adding to your next homemade soup.

Build the lasagna by placing 1 pasta sheet in the simmering water and allow to cook for 3 minutes. Remove from water and put the blanched pasta sheet onto a work surface and pat dry. Continue working to cook the remaining pasta sheets in this manner as you work to build the lasagna.

Top the first cooked sheet with about an eighth of the parsley/ricotta mixture working with an offset spatula to spread evenly. Put 2 tablespoons tomato sauce into the bottom of the prepared loaf pan and spread evenly, then lay the first parsley/ricotta topped pasta sheet on top. Place about 6 postage-stamp-sized pieces of mozzarella cheese about the layer and dollop uncheesed areas with scant teaspoons of sauce in a Jackson Pollack-like manner. Continue building each layer with the remaining ingredients. Top the completed pan of lasagna with more shredded Parmesan cheese.

Cover with foil and bake in a preheated 350° F oven for 30 minutes, then uncover and bake for 10 minutes more. Remove from oven and let cool for at least 15 minutes before cutting and serving. Serve with any remaining (or additional) tomato sauce on the side and garnished with, what else?—a big sprig of fresh parsley.

Parsley as Part of a Healthy Diet

Mediterranean diets became quite popular in the late 1980s largely because of their association with the lowered risk of heart attacks and stroke, particularly in men. The consumption of more vegetables, grains, and fish prepared with better fats and less meat overall, especially red meats, form the keystone of this "new" cuisine. Other than the omnipresent offering of a hummus mixture comprised of most every conceivable bean or vegetable, one could rely that some variation of the Lebanese national dish—Tabbouleh— would be available. This simple but delicious salad is almost always nestled on a meze platter, alongside the bean dips, olives, stuffed grape leaves, yogurts, and flatbreads.

Quinoa Tabbouleh

Authentic tabbouleh is much more an herb salad with a little bit of grain added just for the texture, though many recipes for the dish developed for the North American palate seem to reverse that original concept. The version I offer here is pukka in that it uses lots of parsley yet modern and updated with the use of the ancient grain quinoa, instead of the classic bulgur.

Bulgur is a cereal food made from the cracked, parboiled groat of a hard variety of durum wheat, and if you prefer you can use it in this recipe instead of the quinoa. Choose a coarse ground bulgur at the market and begin by placing 1 cup bulgur in a large bowl and cover with 2 inches of cold water. Let soak for 2 hours or until the bulgur is soft. Drain off any excess water and fluff with a fork.

Serves 6

1 cup quinoa
1 1/4 cups vegetable broth

6 tablespoons lemon juice, fresh, divided
2 cups cherry tomatoes, halved
Kosher salt
2 cups cucumber, peeled and seeded, finely chopped
3 green onions, using all, finely chopped
1 clove garlic, minced
1/3 cup olive oil, extra virgin
Black pepper, freshly ground
2 cups fresh Italian parsley, packed, then chopped
3/4 cup mint, fresh, shredded

Put the quinoa into a mesh strainer and rinse well with cold running water; set aside and allow to drain.

Combine the quinoa, vegetable broth, and 2 tablespoons of the lemon juice in a medium-sized, heavy-bottomed saucepan and place over medium heat. Bring just to a boil, reduce heat to a simmer, cover and cook until all of the liquid is absorbed, about 12 minutes. When done, the grains will appear soft, translucent, and the germ ring will show around the outside edge. Transfer to a shallow platter and spread to cool to room temperature.

Meanwhile, put the tomatoes in a colander and sprinkle lightly with salt. Allow to drain for about 10 minutes.

When the quinoa has cooled, put into a large bowl, add the drained tomatoes, cucumber, green onions, garlic, remaining 4 tablespoons of lemon juice, and the olive oil. Season with salt and freshly ground black pepper to taste and gently toss to combine.

Chill at least 1 hour or until ready to serve. Just before serving, stir in the Italian parsley and the mint.

Parsley as Ingrained Flavor

Martha Ziady, a most amazing and talented home chef, was my chosen mentor when I decided to immerse myself in the flavors of the lower Mediterranean basin, especially those of Lebanon. Martha came highly recommended by a mutual friend who was a teacher at my cooking school in Louisville. It was only natural for me to pick her for my instruction as she was born in Lebanon—Lebanon, Kentucky, that is.

A native Marion Countian, Martha found young and handsome Fermen Ziady, a Lebanese national, during college years spent somewhere along the upper

East Coast. Of course, it was love at first sight or something like that and they married shortly after both garnered their sheepskins. Ferman accepted a great job offer at a large chemical company in Louisville, applied for permanent citizenship, and life together back in Kentucky began.

It wasn't too long before the pangs of hunger for the familiar flavors of home set in and Fermen convinced Martha to make a journey to his homeland, mesh with his relatives, and spend a few months with his mother who agreed to offer an intense introduction to the cultures and cuisine of the land. She stayed on the small family farm near the shores of Tripoli for near six months and absorbed everything possible. I can only assume she was a good student and that the stomach was truly the way to her man's heart as they recently celebrated sixty-five years together, surrounded by a loving, well-fed family in a banquet hall filled with good friends.

One of my favorite dishes is Martha's Lebanese rendition of a Persian variation of the Italian frittata. Known in Arab communities as Kuku Sabzi, it is traditionally served at New Years, symbolizing rebirth (herbs) and fertility (eggs). This is a dish where eggs form the bulk but herbs, in all their glory, are the stars. This recipe highlights the flavor and color of parsley with an assist from a tad of cilantro and a hint of dill.

Green Herb Frittata or Kuku Sabzi. *Karen England*

Green Herb Frittata or Kuku Sabzi

The writer, J.M. Hirsch, recipe chef, Elizabeth Germain, and Christopher Kimball of Milk Street Magazine call this egg dish from Iran an "omelet" but it's actually more like a gluten free, souffléd cake, resembling a green round of skillet-baked cornbread rather than any omelet we Americans can conjure up. Herbal chef Karen England takes this recipe up a notch by adding 3/4 teaspoon ground cardamom, 3/4 teaspoon ground cinnamon, and 1/2 teaspoon ground cumin.

6 large eggs
1 clove garlic, minced
1 tablespoon flour
1/2 teaspoon turmeric powder
1 teaspoon kosher salt
1/2 teaspoon black pepper, freshly ground
6 green onions, using all, chopped
2 cups fresh Italian flat leaf parsley, well-packed, then chopped fine
1/2 cup fresh cilantro, well-packed, then chopped fine
1/2 cup fresh dill, well-packed, then chopped fine
1/4 cup walnuts, chopped
1/4 cup currants (or dried cranberries)
2 tablespoons butter, unsalted
Yogurt, for topping

Serves 6

In a large mixing bowl whisk together the eggs, garlic, flour, turmeric, salt, and black pepper until well blended. Add the green onions, parsley, cilantro, dill, walnuts, and currants and mix in well.

Place a 10- or 12-inch cast iron skillet or similar oven-proof pan over medium heat, add the butter and swirl to coat the pan. Pour the egg mixture into the skillet using a spatula to spread the ingredients out evenly. Cook until the egg starts to set around the edges of the skillet, about 2 minutes.

Put the skillet into a preheated 400° F oven and bake until the eggs are completely set, about 8 minutes. Check by cutting a small slit in the center; it should be firm. Remove from oven and let sit for a few minutes to completely firm up.

Serve it hot, room temperature, or even cold, cut into wedges and accompanied by a nice dollop of fresh, tangy yogurt.

Parsley as a Side Dish

While a great steak, a slice of meatloaf, a chop of lamb, or a tasty fillet of fish is always welcome on my plate, what I really come to the dinner table for are the side dishes. I'm not a vegetarian but I could be one—except for bacon. The most notable cookbook of the few I have written is all about the wonderful world of sides and which is best to accompany any meal—it is entitled *Go Withs*. The book has been out-of-print for a while, but it can occasionally be found at online used book stores for a reasonable fee if you care to give it a hunt.

Grandmother Vetrice, who was the main cook in our house during my adolescent years, would always nab me as I returned home from school or summer play, apron me up and say that she had made a chicken casserole or some other delicious entree and that she needed my help to prepare a few sides to *go with* the main event. So my love of and quest for a great side dish was instilled at an early age and lingers on.

This preparation for a well-herbed, mixed grain pilaf should please the most discriminating diner. It is a vibrantly green gem to behold on platter, plate, and palate.

Verdant Rice and Barley Pilaf

This recipe can be made successfully using vegetable broth if you want to keep it vegetarian or chicken broth if you want to give it a lighter taste. I like the use of the beef broth as it gives the final pilaf a more robust, dimensional taste.

Serves 6

1/4 cup extra virgin olive oil
1 cup long grain rice
1/2 cup quick-cooking, pearled barley
3/4 cup fresh Italian flat leaf parsley, well-packed, then chopped fine
1 teaspoon sesame oil
3 cups beef broth
2 green onions, using all, sliced thin

Kosher salt
Freshly ground black pepper

Heat the olive oil in a large, heavy-bottomed saucepan over medium heat. Add the rice and barley, stir well to coat and cook for 5 minutes, stirring occasionally. Add the parsley, reserving 1 tablespoon, then the sesame oil and the beef broth. Bring to a boil.

Reduce heat to low, cover tightly and continue to cook for 15 minutes. Remove from heat but do not open or remove the lid and let stand for 15 minutes more. Season with salt and freshly ground black pepper to taste. Add the green onions and the reserved parsley, mixing and fluffing the pilaf with a fork. Serve immediately.

Another *go with* vegetable that works well to transcend its accompanying herb is green beans. Ubiquitous because of their general appeal to a wide spectrum of eaters, green beans are an excellent choice prepared in most any manner. My grandmother, a gardener of the succulent Kentucky Wonder variety, would either cook them with copious amounts of black pepper-studded salt pork to within an inch of their delicious life or can them as a pickle with loads of mustard seeds and dill. Her framed collection of county fair blue ribbons for those dilled green beans is a family heirloom.

I didn't learn the joys of green beans cooked to a perfect al dente until my culinary school days. And while I can really enjoy the flavors of "country-style" beans when seeking a comfort meal, most often I choose to prepare them in the manner of the French—steamed or parboiled until just tender and, if not using as a salad, succumbing to a quick, well-seasoned skillet sauté.

I developed one of my favorite green bean recipes from a recipe/technique shared by my friend Ann Willan on one of her many visits to my Kentucky cooking school. Ann was the founder of Ecole de Cuisine/La Varenne in Paris in 1975. La Varenne, named for a famous old Burgundian chef, was one of the first professional cooking schools in all of France. The school quickly garnered great acclaim and attracted students from around the world. It moved from Paris to the Chateau du Fey in Burgundy in 1990 and sadly closed with Ann's retirement in 2007.

Italian Parsley Watercolor. *Gail Wood Miller*

Green Beans Dressed for Summer

Serves 8

2 pounds green beans, trimmed
6 tablespoons extra virgin olive oil
8 large shallots, sliced thin
5 tablespoons white wine vinegar
2 teaspoons Dijon mustard, coarse grained
3 green onions, using all, chopped fine
3/4 cup fresh Italian flat leaf parsley, packed well, then chopped
Zest of 1 lemon
Kosher salt
White pepper, freshly ground
1/2 cup pine nuts, toasted or sliced/slivered almonds

Bring a large pot of cold water to the boil, add 1 tablespoon of salt, and when the water has returned to the boil, add the green beans. Reduce heat to medium-high and cook until just tender, about 8 minutes. Pour into a colander, drain, and immediately rinse with very cold water to stop the cooking process and set the color. Or alternately drop the cooked beans into a large pan of iced water. Drain well and set aside.

In a medium-sized, nonreactive skillet, heat 2 tablespoons olive oil over medium heat. Add the shallots and cook, stirring often, until the shallots are nearly caramelized, about 6 to 8 minutes. Add the vinegar and allow it to reduce by half, stirring the pan often and well.

Remove from heat and allow to cool for a few minutes. Scrape the contents of the pan into a large work bowl, add the mustard and the remaining olive oil and whisk well. Add the green onions, parsley and lemon zest and mix well. Season with salt and pepper to taste.

Add the green beans, and toss well. Put onto a serving plate and sprinkle the pine nuts over. Top with a beautiful large sprig of parsley. Serve at room temperature.

Parsley in Sauces

While a perfectly grilled steak, ideally sautéed chop or a flawless baked fillet of fish can be wonderfully satisfying served direct from chef to diner, the addition of a well-conceived sauce can take most any offering to new dimensions of culinary sophistication and flavor.

The following three recipes are a true herbal saucier's apprentice. Use any one of them with a deft hand and word will quickly spread of your kitchen mastery.

Chimichurri Sauce II

Chimichurri is an Argentinean sauce or marinade (some say it originated in Uruguay) typically made with Italian flat leaf parsley. Lots of it. It is a popular sauce served with most any grilled meat in Latin American countries. The origin of its name is not quite clear, though one story says that the name comes from an Irishman named Jimmy who had developed a curry—Jimmy's Curry—while in the country to help fight for Argentine independence. Or much less romantically, was in the region developing a meat export business. The sauce can be spicy hot with added chile flakes (like this recipe) or the heat can be toned down by using only half the chile amount or even left out entirely. The red wine vinegar and olive oil work to smooth the consistency, mellow the herb flavor, and infuse the meat.

Serves 4

1/2 cup extra virgin olive oil
2 tablespoons red wine vinegar
1 lemon, zest of and juice of half
1 large bunch fresh Italian flat leaf parsley, chopped fine
1 tablespoon fresh oregano, chopped
1 large shallot, minced
1 clove garlic, minced
About 1 teaspoon red pepper flakes

Combine the olive oil, red wine vinegar, lemon zest and juice, parsley, oregano, shallot, garlic, and red pepper flakes in a mixing bowl and whisk until well combined. Let the mixture stand for at least 1 hour before using.

Use as a meat marinade or a side sauce for most any grilled meat, fish or vegetable. Refrigerate any remaining sauce and use within a week or so.

English Parsley Sauce

A product of traditional British kitchens, classic Parsley Sauce is a most versatile and useful condiment that works particularly well with fish and pasta. It is a variation of the classic Bechamel Sauce and surprisingly easy to make. Note: this sauce can be tailored to fit its use and inclusion in specific dishes by changing the vegetable broth to beef, chicken or seafood broth if that change would add additional dimension to the final dish.

Serves 6

2 tablespoons butter, unsalted
2 tablespoons flour, all-purpose
1 cup milk, whole, at room temperature
1 cup vegetable broth, at room temperature
3/4 cup Italian flat leaf parsley, well-packed, then chopped
Kosher salt
White pepper, freshly ground

Melt the butter in a medium-sized, heavy-bottomed pan over low heat, whisk in the flour, stirring about a 2 minutes to form a roux.

Slowly pour the milk into the roux and continue stirring and cooking for 1 minute more, then stir in the vegetable stock and continue to cook, stirring frequently for about 4 minutes or until the sauce has become thickened and creamy.

Stir in the parsley and season with salt and freshly ground white pepper.

Parsley Pesto with Pistachios

Back in the early 1980s the word "pesto" was as foreign a term to most non-Italian Americans as other culinary technique terms that now float easily off the tongues of novice cooks infused with knowledge from the avalanche of cable and television food shows like Top Chef, Dueling Skillets, Chopped and the like.

Pesto—traditionally a combination of the herb basil, a few sprigs parsley, lots of garlic, Parmesan cheese, pine nuts, and good olive oil pounded and blended to a smooth pulverization—is an ultimate comfort food. It freezes well, thaws quickly, and has a multitude of uses by enlightened and creative cooks. Add pesto to cooked pasta for a quick meal, to soups or stews as a flavor booster, spread under the skin of chicken breasts or thighs when roasting or grilling, slather on pizza dough as a base sauce, or fold into your favorite dough for a fantastic bread.

This recipe takes pesto to the next level and is offered here to stir your creative juices into wondering what other herb combinations could be tried to make such an ever useful sauce/marinade always at the ready to enhance your family and company meals for years to come. Enjoy!

2 cups fresh Italian flat leaf parsley, well-packed
1 small shallot, chopped
3/4 cup Asiago cheese, freshly grated
1/4 cup pistachio nuts
1/2 cup extra virgin olive oil
1 teaspoon white pepper, freshly ground

Makes about 1 cup

Combine the parsley, shallot, cheese, and pistachios in a food processor or blender. Process to mix; with the machine running, slowly add the olive oil. Season to taste with the white pepper and continue processing until a fine paste is formed.

Let stand at least 15 minutes before using. Use as a sauce or condiment for most anything. Dress pasta, rub meats, baste chickens, top fish, add to breads and crusts or dollop in soups and stews. It is a powerhouse of flavor and usefullness. On top of that, it freezes well.

References

Hirsch, J.M. "Persian Herb Omelet." *Christopher Kimball's Milk Street Magazine*, March-April 2017.

Lacy Italian Parsley. *Skye Suter*

Known as the *HerbMeister*, **Stephen Lee** has enjoyed a diverse culinary career consistently interwoven with his love of herbs. He is the author of five books, including *About 8 Herbs* and *Go Withs*. He founded and operated The Cookbook Cottage, an internationally known source for rare and out-of-print cookbooks, and Kentucky's first and only cooking school for fifteen years.

Twice Chairman of the Cooking Schools and Teachers Committee of the International Association of Culinary Professionals, Stephen recently retired as the director of the Daily Lunch Program for the Homeless for the Archdiocese of Louisville. He is Superintendent of the Culinary Department of the Kentucky State Fair, a licensed and active Auctioneer/Appraiser in both Indiana and Kentucky, a Board Member of the IHA Foundation, and an honest-to-goodness Kentucky Colonel. Learn more at www.herbmeister. com.

Parsley Pixie. *Skye Suter*

Parsley for the Garden and Kitchen: Herb of the Year 2021

Theresa Mieseler

Parsley was patiently waiting and in 2021 it is the International Herb Association's Herb of the Year™. It is an herb well known to seasoned as well as novice gardeners. Parsley, a biennial, is in the Apiaceae family. It is easy to grow, does well in full sun, prefers a well-drained soil, and loves to be used by being kept trimmed during the growing season.

Seeds are sown ten to twelve weeks before transplanting into the garden. It was many years ago I realized that parsley seeds need to be soaked before sowing and this goes for all varieties of parsley. Without a pre-soak, seeds show poor germination and longer sprouting times. The night before sowing, I soak seeds in hot water, strain the next morning, slightly dry on paper towels, and sow in a soilless medium. Unlike other seeds that require bottom heat, parsley does not and germinates better without it. Seeds germinate within ten to fourteen days and are ready for transplanting into three-inch containers in two weeks. Parsley can be planted into the garden earlier than tender herbs, such as basil, since it is a cold-resistant plant. In Minnesota, I plant basil around May 20 but parsley in early May. I prefer to savor the flavor of parsley by chopping and freezing it for use in the off season.

Parsley is an attractive herb not only for kitchen use but also for the butterflies that lay their eggs on specific host plants. The swallowtail caterpillar is found on parsley, dill, and fennel plants. Large flat rocks with a hollow space for water attract butterflies. Plant extra parsley for the butterflies.

Parsley is well suited to container gardening, and it grows well with thyme, oregano, rosemary, and sage in a container or strawberry jar. Make sure your planting medium drains rapidly but retains enough moisture to keep the roots evenly moist. Purchase a good quality potting mixture or make your own from equal parts of sand, loamy garden soil, and peat moss. As far as fertilizing plants, it's a good idea to use a dilute liquid fertilizer with every other watering. Liquid fish emulsion or an organic fertilizer is a great plant booster. Parsley varieties are curly leaved, flat leaf (Italian), and Hamburg root.

Curled Parsley

Petroselinum crispum var. *crispum*

A mild-flavored parsley that has uniform height and an upright growing habit with sturdy, long stems. Once cut, it quickly regrows for additional parsley crops. Varieties to grow: 'Moss curled', 'Wega', and 'Krausa'.

Flat Leaf Parsley

P. crispum var. *neapolitanum*

Flat leaf or Italian parsley is my favorite parsley to use in cooking. It has a pleasant flavor to add to any cuisine. Cut it often in the garden and it will reward you by growing back time after time. Here's a favorite recipe I use on my salads with Italian parsley. Varieties to choose: 'Giant of Italy', 'Peione'.

Italian Parsley. *Theresa Mieseler*

Basil and Parsley Vinaigrette Dressing

Serves 6

1/2 cup extra virgin olive oil
1/4 cup freshly grated Parmesan cheese
1/4 cup apple cider vinegar
1 large clove garlic, chopped
2 tablespoons coarsely snipped fresh sweet basil
2 tablespoons coarsely chopped fresh parsley, curly or Italian
1 tablespoon chopped fresh chives
1 teaspoon honey
1 teaspoon dry mustard
Salt and pepper to taste

Combine all of the above ingredients in food processor or blender. Refrigerate any leftover dressing. I use it to dress kale, arugula, radicchio, small leafy greens, and edible flowers.

Herbs in salad dressing: chives, basil, curly parsley. *Theresa Mieseler*

Parsley Root, Hamburg

P. crispum tuberosum

Root parsley is delicious in soups, roasted vegetables, and stews. The six- to eight-inch roots are smaller than parsnips. Roots are pale, less yellow than parsnips, and slender. Eat roots raw in salads or cooked with other root vegetables. The roots are commonly used in Bulgaria, Poland, and Russia. My friends in Poland use it as a vegetable in salads. Roots mature in eighty to ninety days. 'Arat' parsley, available from Johnny's Seeds, has a mild celery flavor. I wait for a frost before harvesting the parsley roots in fall.

Hamburg Parsley. *Theresa Mieseler*

Hamburg Parsley Soup

Note: You can use 3 Hamburg parsley and 3 parsnips instead of all parsley roots.

Serves 2 as a meal, 4 as a starter

4 tablespoons olive oil
1 medium red onion, sliced
6 parsley roots, peeled and cut into one-inch slices
2 small carrots, peeled and cut into one-inch slices
3 stalks celery, cut into one-inch slices
6 sprigs fresh thyme, minced
6 sprigs oregano, minced
1/2 teaspoon salt
1/2 teaspoon pepper
1 quart chicken broth
Splash apple cider vinegar or white dry wine
2 tablespoons Italian parsley, minced

Preheat oven to 400° F.

Mix onion, parsley roots, carrots, celery, thyme, oregano, salt, and pepper in a bowl with olive oil. Place on a cookie sheet and heat in oven for about 25 to 30 minutes. When tender, purée in a blender with chicken broth, garlic, and apple cider vinegar or white wine. Reheat and garnish with chopped Italian parsley and serve with crusty bread.

Theresa Mieseler and husband, Jim, founded Shady Acres Herb Farm in 1977 where they grew both common and unique herbs plus vegetables—heirlooms were a specialty. Theresa is a lifetime member of the Herb Society of America and in 2010 was awarded the Nancy Putnam Howard Award for Excellence in Horticulture. As an International Herb Association member, Theresa served as vice-president and board member. In 1999, Theresa introduced 'Shady Acres' Rosemary. As of 2016, they no longer grow plants for sale. Since then, Shady Acres Herb Farm has been moving in a different direction where now the focus is Theresa teaching others about growing plants through a monthly newsletter, presentations, and events. Visit them at www.shadyacres.com. In March, 2019, Theresa's book, *Beyond Rosemary, Basil, and Thyme*, was self-published.

Strawberry and Parsley Summer Salad. *Cooper T. Murray*

Partnering with Parsley

Cooper T. Murray

During my educational cooking shows, I share my love of cooking with fresh herbs. Honestly, parsley has not too often been the featured herb. But, parsley is always there like an old friend, supporting the showcased herb. With parsley as the International Herb Association Herb of the Year™ for 2021, it makes me realize that I really do use parsley as the main herb in many of my recipes. It is indeed a favorite and appreciated.

Flat leaf and curly parsley will always be part of my garden. Snipping fresh parsley with its refreshing scent is enjoyable and uplifting. While parsley is readily available to everyone to use in their cooking with grocery stores offering parsley throughout the year, there's nothing that compares to fresh picked parsley bursting with flavor.

Eating a healthy diet and appreciating fresh nutritious recipes, I strive to create recipes that nourish our bodies and also taste delicious. Parsley's leaves are silky and light while the stems are tender and should not be ignored. What a wonderful herb we celebrate. Here's to parsley!

Strawberry and Parsley Summer Salad

When strawberries are in season and fresh parsley is thriving in my garden, this salad has become a favorite. It is a bright, beautiful, and healthy salad bursting with flavor. Make ahead of time for a party or picnic, undressed, keeping in the refrigerator for up to 6 hours. Strawberries are fantastic, but try peaches or other summer fruit for a delightful change.

Serves 4

Salad Vinaigrette

1/4 cup sliced strawberries
4 tablespoons olive oil
3 tablespoons balsamic vinegar
1 green onion, thinly sliced with scissors
1 tablespoon lemon juice
1/4 teaspoon salt

Salad

10 ounces arugula-spinach mixture
3/4 cup flat leaf parsley leaves and tender stems
1 pint strawberries, hulled and quartered
3 baby cucumbers, sliced (Persian or home grown)
1 pint cherry tomatoes, sliced in half
1/4 small red onion, finely sliced
1/2 cup crumbled feta cheese

For the vinaigrette, combine all the ingredients in a blender or food processor. Blend until smooth and creamy. Place in a small jar and refrigerate until ready to use. Dressing can be made up to 3 days ahead.

Place the salad mixture in a large bowl or platter. Top with salad ingredients. Before serving, drizzle with dressing

Keto Fathead Parsley Rolls. *Cooper T. Murray*

Keto Fathead Parsley Rolls

With the Keto diet being so popular, I try to create recipes that bring the comfort of real bread. This recipe does just that in a short amount of time. Using almond flour keeps the carbs low. This recipe with flat leaf parsley is a favorite. They are great with butter or as rolls for petite sandwiches.

Serves 4

2 ounces cream cheese
3/4 cup shredded mozzarella
1 egg
1/4 teaspoon garlic powder
1/3 cup almond flour
2 teaspoons baking powder
1/2 cup shredded cheddar cheese
1/4 cup, chopped flat leaf parsley
Cooking spray or olive oil for parchment paper

Preheat the oven to 425° F. In a small bowl, add cream cheese and mozzarella. Microwave on high for 30 seconds. Stir to blend.

In a separate bowl, whisk egg until beaten. Add garlic powder, almond flour, and baking powder. Mix well. Dough will be sticky.

Return the cream cheese and mozzarella mixture to the microwave. Microwave for 20 seconds. Stir well. Add to the dough mixture. Stir in cheddar cheese and parsley.

Spoon dough onto plastic wrap. Dust top with a sprinkle of almond flour. Fold the plastic wrap over the dough and gently shape into a ball. Cover and refrigerate for 30 minutes.

Remove from the refrigerator. Unwrap the dough and cut into 4 pieces. Roll each section into a ball. Cut in half. This will create the top half and bottom half of the roll.

Place cut side down on parchment paper on a cookie sheet sprayed with cooking spray. Bake for 8 minutes. Flip rolls and bake for another 4 minutes. Serve warm.

Parsley-Poached Chicken Salad

Poaching chicken seems to have gone out of fashion. It really is a fantastic way to add the flavors of fresh herbs and citrus resulting in deliciously moist chicken. This is a two-part recipe. Fresh parsley adds the perfect depth to poached chicken. The flavorful stems simmer while the tender leaves accent the chicken salad. Living in the South, chicken salad is a way of life. A scoop of Parsley Chicken Salad on baby greens or a biscuit is wonderful. My chicken salad is simple, allowing the flavor of parsley to stand out.

Serves 6

Poached Chicken

4 skinless, boneless chicken breasts
1 lemon, sliced into 1/2 inch slices
Stems and leaves from 1 bunch of parsley, curly or flat leaf
1 tablespoon salt
1 tablespoon ground pepper
5 cups water

Add all of the ingredients to a medium saucepan. Bring to a slight boil. Turn down the heat and simmer for 12 minutes. Remove from heat and place chicken on a plate to cool. Refrigerate the chicken if not preparing the salad right away.

Parsley Chicken Salad

1 1/2 cups to 2 cups mayonnaise
2 teaspoons Dijon mustard
4 poached chicken breasts, finely chopped
1/4 cup fresh parsley, chopped
1 teaspoon salt
1 teaspoon ground pepper

Add mayonnaise and Dijon mustard to a mixing bowl. Stir to blend. Add chicken, parsley, salt and pepper. Mix well. Add additional mayonnaise if needed. Serve on a bed of lettuce or a scoop on a sandwich.

Poached chicken with parsley and lemon. *Cooper T. Murray*

Parsley-Poached Chicken Salad. *Cooper T. Murray*

Parmesan Parsley Roasted Cauliflower

Cauliflower has become a superstar in the vegetable world these last few years. It is low-carb and so versatile. Cauliflower is the perfect side dish. Your friends and family will not miss the potatoes tonight. The cheese adds depth and deliciousness to this simple dish.

Serves 4 to 6

1 medium head cauliflower
4 tablespoons olive oil
1/2 teaspoon salt
1/2 teaspoon pepper
1/2 teaspoon garlic powder
1 cup grated Parmesan cheese
1 cup shredded Italian blend cheese
1 cup fresh parsley, chopped

Preheat the oven to 350° F. Wash and remove the outer leaves from the cauliflower. Remove the hard core. Cut the head into small florets. Place cauliflower in a large bowl. Drizzle with olive oil. Add salt and pepper. Toss well to coat cauliflower. Place in a medium baking pan. Bake for 20 minutes. Remove from the oven. Sprinkle with Parmesan, Italian cheese blend, and parsley. Return to the oven and cook 5 more minutes.

Parmesan Parsley Roasted Cauliflower. *Cooper T. Murray*

Parsley Butter Pan Seared Scallops. *Cooper T. Murray*

Parsley Butter Pan Seared Scallops

We are all very busy with our jobs, our homes, our gardens, and our family. Cooking simply with a few ingredients is ideal. Lemon, butter, and parsley really work well with scallops. I use large scallops, but small bay scallops can be substituted. These scallops are perfect with a thin pasta or served alongside a garden salad. Both flat leaf or curly parsley are suitable.

Serves 4

12 large scallops, thawed
4 tablespoons olive oil
1/2 teaspoon salt
1/2 teaspoon ground pepper
4 tablespoons unsalted butter, cubed
Zest of 1 lemon
Juice of 1/2 lemon
1/2 cup fresh parsley chopped

Place scallops on layers of paper towels. Cover with more paper towels. Let them rest on the paper towels for 10 minutes to absorb moisture. Remove paper towels. Sprinkle scallops with salt and pepper. Heat olive oil in a cast iron pan over medium high heat. Place scallops in the pan. Cook for 3 minutes to sear. Flip scallops and cook for 3 more minutes. (I prefer my scallops golden brown.)

Reduce heat to medium. Add butter to the pan. Swirl the pan to melt the butter. Spoon melted butter over scallops. Add lemon zest and lemon juice. Top with parsley. Remove from heat and serve.

Japanese Parsley Cheesecake. *Cooper T. Murray*

Japanese Parsley Cheesecake

I have always been fond of fresh herbs in desserts. Herbs bring desserts to a whole new level, adding that je ne sais quoi. My friend who owns a Japanese restaurant served this surprising dessert at a private event. Thankfully, he shared the unique recipe. It is a light cheesecake with a vibrant color provided by parsley. Surprise your guests as they enjoy this charming dessert.

Serves 8 to 10

1/2 cup unbleached all-purpose flour
3 tablespoons cornstarch
1/2 teaspoon salt
1/2 cup whole milk
1 cup flat leaf parsley, finely chopped
8-ounces cream cheese
1/4 cup unsalted butter
1 tablespoon lemon juice
6 eggs, separated
3/4 cup sugar

Preheat the oven to 325° F with the oven rack placed in the middle. Line an 8-inch square baking pan with parchment paper, allowing it to hang over all four sides.

In a bowl combine the flour, cornstarch, and salt. Set aside. In a blender, puree the milk and parsley until smooth.

Over medium heat, using a double boiler, melt the cream cheese, butter, and lemon juice. Stir the mixture constantly until smooth and creamy. Remove from heat. Add the egg yolks and parsley to cream cheese. Whisk in the flour-cornstarch mixture.

In another bowl, whisk the egg whites with an electric mixer until soft peaks form. Add the sugar gradually while whisking until stiff peaks form. Carefully fold the egg whites into the batter using the whisk. Transfer to the baking pan.

Place the cake pan in a larger baking pan and add hot water to the larger pan. The water should be about 1/3 the way up the sides.

Bake for 1 hour and 15 minutes. Remove the cake from the double boiler. Let cool for 2 hours. Cover and refrigerate until completely chilled, about 6 hours.

Cut into squares to serve. Japanese Parsley Cheesecake can be made up to 2 days ahead.

Tamara "Cooper" Murray, BA, MA is a graduate of Nazareth College and the University of Kansas. Originally from Binghamton, New York, and living for many years in Colorado, she now calls Alabama her home and enjoys the long growing season of the South. Cooper's influence came from her grandmother who immigrated to the United States and became a cook in New York City for the wealthy. Cooper furthered her culinary knowledge working at country clubs and restaurants. She creates recipes that highlight herbs and has written for numerous magazines and publications. Cooper's fondness for herbs and cooking led her to develop Organic Herbal Cooking, Inc. Her company offers motivational and educational cooking events in the Southeast. She writes Organic Herbal Cooking's blog and shares the benefits of cooking with herbs in simple healthy cooking. Any conversation with her usually leads to talking about fresh herbs! Not a day goes by that Cooper is not savoring the benefits of cooking with herbs. Contact Cooper at organicherbalcooking.com or coopertmurray@gmail.com.

That Popular Parsley Salad Dressing

Diann Nance

Here is a flash from the past. Everybody in the 50s and 60s knew about Green Goddess Dressing, and it was quite a favorite. Now, I think few people are even aware of it; however, there are still many variations of the recipe available. This one I've adapted from a cooking-show host and internationally-known caterer of that period, Phila Hach. (Look for her on *Wikipedia*.) She claimed that this recipe originated in the South Pacific. Try it; it's delicious on more than just vegetables. Anchovy paste is available at grocery stores and on line.

Phila's Green Goddess Dressing

Serves 6 to 8

1 cup sour cream
1/2 cup dried parsley
1/2 cup spring onions or chives
1/2 cup celery
1/2 cup chopped cucumbers
1 teaspoon lemon juice
1 teaspoon garlic salt
1 1.6 ounce-tube anchovy paste
1 cup mayonnaise
1 teaspoon dried tarragon
Salt and pepper

Process parsley, spring onions and celery in a food processor. Then mix all ingredients together in a glass bowl and store in the refrigerator. Shake before using and serve over vegetables or salad.

Bella loves these parsley dog biscuits. *Diann Nance*

Pets Love Parsley, Too

Diann Nance

My dog Bella loves these biscuits. I have added much more parsley and some berries to this recipe, adapted from Jerry Traunfeld's *The Herbal Kitchen*. Parsley is good for getting rid of doggy breath. It is also a rich source of vitamins and minerals, so not only is parsley good for people, it's good for your canine best friend.

Good Dog Biscuits

1 3/4 cups rolled oats
1 3/4 cups whole wheat flour
1/4 cup dry nutritional yeast
1 cup parsley sprigs, gently packed
1/2 cup peanut butter
1/2 cup blueberries, blackberries, or raspberries
1 egg
1 cup water

Preheat the oven to 275° F.

Blend the oats, flour, yeast, and parsley in a food processor until well mixed. Add the peanut butter and process until combined. Add the egg, berries, and water and process until the dough forms a firm ball that spins around the blade.

Place the dough on a well floured board and knead briefly. Pinch off a piece of dough (a size corresponding to the size of your dog), and roll it into a cylinder. Form it into a bone shape, pressing a fingertip into both ends to create sockets. Arrange the biscuits on a parchment paper-lined baking sheet. Bake the biscuits for about 2 hours, or until lightly browned and quite dry. Cool and store in an airtight container.

Flat Italian Parsley. *Richters*

Diann Nance, born and raised on a farm in north central Texas, is presently living and growing herbs among the beautiful rolling hills of north central Tennessee. After a forty-year teaching career which included time spent in Texas, Taiwan, Germany, and finally Tennessee, she realized a long-held dream of starting a plant-growing business. Although Diann is now retired from the business of herbs, she still grows and uses herbs on a regular basis. Her interest in herbs and their uses in our daily lives can be attributed to her mother and grandmother, who loved plants and sharing their knowledge of herbs and plants in general. Diann continues this tradition by growing plants, conducting workshops, and demonstrating the uses of herbs. She is a Master Gardener, a member of the Beachaven Garden Club, The Herb Society of America, and the International Herb Association. She a lifelong learner and may be contacted at dinance40@gmail.com.

Parsley Particulars

Karen O'Brien

Parsley is an herb that everyone knows but most everyone doesn't really care about. We have grown up in the era of "the parsley garnish," a blob of green to decorate the plate in even the smallest of restaurants. I do remember reading about that garnish, back in the seventies, that it was actually pretty good for you to eat it, rather than just let it decorate the plate. It was a kind of revelation to me, and probably my first foray into what herbs can really do for you. I ended up learning that parsley was so much more than an ornament.

As L.Young Correthers penned:

> *The modern use of parsley*
> > *Is to place her rather sparsely*
> *As an ornament, for any kind of food.*
> > *But when the Ancients found her*
> *With violets they bound her*
> > *And wore her to banquets as a snood.*
> *She makes a charming frilly hedge*
> > *And neatly trims the border's edge.*

Parsley is in the Apiaceae family, along with many other umbels such as dill, fennel, and Queen Anne's lace. The word Apiaceae is derived from the Greek word for celery, and parsley's botanical name, *Petroselinum*, comes from *petros* (meaning rock) and *selinon* (meaning celery). There are three main varieties of parsley: *crispum*—the curly type which is the most ornamental; *neapolitanum*— flat-leaved and more favored for cooking; and *tuberosum*—root parsley, in which the root rather than the leaves are used. It is a true biennial, in that the seeds do not occur until the second year, but most everyone grows it as an annual. It can take a lot of cutting, and continues to set leaves until frost.

Parsley is notoriously bad at germinating, and is said that the seed needs to go to the devil seven times before it will appear. It can take four to six weeks to germinate. Some soak the seed overnight to encourage better germination by softening the seed coat. Sowing radish seeds along with the parsley is a good way to mark the row, as the radishes come up quickly. When you harvest the radishes, it is usually time to thin the parsley, so two chores can be accomplished at the same time.

As to its benefits, parsley is high in vitamins, especially A, K, and C. By weight, it has three times as much vitamin C as oranges. The flat leaved types are higher in vitamin C than the curly types. It is a good source of chlorophyll, and so is very effective as a breath sweetener. In ancient times it was thought to negate the effects of wine and thus prevent inebriation. In fact, the Greeks and Romans did not eat parsley but rather wore it.

> *At Sparta's Palace twenty beauteous mayds,*
> *The pride of Greece, fresh garlands crowned their heads*
> *With hyacinths and twining parsley drest,*
> *Graced joyful Menelaus' marriage feast.*
> -Theocritus

Dedicated to Persephone, parsley was used in Grecian funeral rites and to adorn graves. It was said to have sprung from the blood of Archemorus, a Greek hero, and became known as a forerunner of death. Interestingly, it was also used for crowning victors in the Isthmian games and Hercules supposedly used it in the first garland he wore. It symbolizes "festivity" and so it would be appropriate as a victory wreath or adornment at a banquet.

Parsley is one of the many plants preferred by the black swallowtail caterpillar, *Papilio polyxenes asterius*. It is loved by rabbits, who will often decimate your planting of it. But it is said to be toxic to small birds and parrots, so beware of feeding it to any caged birds. Sheep also like it, and it has been fed to them as a preventative to foot rot. Ancient warriors fed it to their chariot horses, believing it would help with their speed and endurance

There are many superstitions surrounding parsley. Victorian girls were admonished never to cut it, as that would bring bad luck in love. Nor could they give it away, lest they give away their own luck. The only way to obtain it was to steal it—so what could a proper Victorian maid do? Parsley planted inside the house would bring death, and planting it on Good Friday was recommended to ensure a good crop. Pregnant women were thought to have more success in planting it. When it finally came up, often erratically, it was believed that the devil had taken his share. It was unlucky to transplant it (most likely due to its large taproot) and, if the plant flourished, it meant the woman of the house was in charge.

Though the ancients did not use it as food, parsley came to be used medicinally. Hildegard of Bingen (1098–1179) recommended it for heart, spleen, and sick stomachs (along with fennel and soapwort), stones (paired with saxifrage, both good for "breaking"), and even paralysis, as an ointment applied to the affected part. The English botanist John Gerard (1545–1612) claimed it destroyed poisons since it had the power to overcome strong smells such as garlic. Nicholas Culpepper (1616–1654) considered it one of the five opening roots, and it has been used since the time of Claudius Galenus (129–200) as a remedy for obstructions. Thomas Hill, in the 1577 printing of *The Gardener's Labyrinth*, claimed it "helpeth the biting of a madde Dogge". A decoction of bruised parsley seeds was used against the plague, and in France parsley was mixed with snails and pounded into an ointment to treat scrofulous swellings. Parsley tea was used for rheumatism (acting on the kidneys and helping to release toxins) and parsley water was taken to soothe flatulence and stomach pain. *The Toilet of Flora* (originally printed in 1779) contains the following recipe to prevent baldness using parsley.

A powder to Prevent Baldnefs.

Powder your head with powdered Parfley Seed, at night, once in three or four months, and the hair will never fall off.

Today parsley is used as for its carminative, tonic, and aperient properties, but chiefly as a diuretic. The leaves soothe swollen or irritated eyes, and a poultice of bruised leaves can relieve the itch and sting of insects. Some use it as a hair rinse, and the seeds may be used to darken the hair color and eliminate dandruff.

Most of us today will use parsley along with other herbs, rather than by itself in recipes. It blends well with lots of other herbs. I found this "delightful" recipe in *Delightes for Ladies* by Hugh Platt, first published in 1609:

To boile Sparrowes or Larkes.

Take two ladles full of mutton broth, a little whole mace, put into it a peece of fweet butter, and handfull of Parfly being picked, feafon it with fugar, veriuice, and a little pepper.

No directions on how this is cooked, but a lady in that day would know just how to do that!

If a strong beverage is what you prefer, then this recipe for parsley wine may suit your needs. It comes from *Herb Lore for Housewives* (1938):

Parsley Wine

Take ½ lb. of Parsley, 1 gallon of water, 3 ½ lb. sugar, two Oranges, two Lemons, ½ oz. yeast, some Raisins, a large slice of toast, and ½ oz. white root Ginger.

Gather the Parsley when it is dry—wash it and place in pan with the water. Bring to the boil and simmer gently for half an hour. Strain. Place the Oranges and Lemons, sliced, with the sugar and bruised Ginger, in a bowl; pour the liquid over these and stir until the sugar is dissolved. Allow this to get luke-warm, then add the yeast spread on a slice of toast. Leave to ferment six or seven days. Skim and strain before bottling. Into each bottle, put two large, juicy split Raisins. Keep the beverage over the harsh period, when it will work clear. As the fine sediment sinks to the bottom of the bottles pour the clear liquid into clean bottles.

In researching this article, I looked at numerous books, many of them cookbooks. Many of Adelma Simmons' books contain recipes using parsley; in fact, some of her books include the use of parsley in over 50 percent of the recipes. But it is usually in conjunction with other herbs that I think parsley really does play nicely with others. We should probably use parsley more—its benefits are clear and it's an easy herb to obtain.

I did find a clipped recipe from a newspaper tucked into one of my books, no doubt placed there by the previous owner, with no idea of where or when it was written. But I think I will have to try it, if only because it sounds intriguing and who knew fried parsley was a thing? And isn't everything really good fried?

Fresh herbs for bouquet garni: rosemary, thyme, parsley, sage, savory, and bay.
Pat Kenny

Fried Parsley

Yields about 6 cups

6 cups loosely packed parsley
Oil for deep frying
Salt

If the parsley has any trace of sand or soil, it should be washed. To do this, rinse in several changes of cold water and shake off the excess moisture, using a salad basket. Pat dry with clean cloth or paper toweling.

Heat the oil and fry the parsley, a handful at a time, using a slotted spoon to see that the parsley cooks evenly in the oil. When done, it will be dark green or greenish black, and crisp. Drain on absorbent toweling. Sprinkle with salt before serving.

References

Campbell, Mary Mason. *A Basket of Herbs: A Book of American Sentiments*. The Stephen Greene Press, 1983.

Foster, Gertrude B. *Herbs for Every Garden*. E.P. Dutton & Co., 1973.

Fox, Helen Morgenthau. *Gardening with Herbs for Flavor and Fragrance*. Macmillan Co., 1933.

Grieve, Maude. *A Modern Herbal, Vol. 11*. Harcourt, Brace & Co.,1931.

Hill, Thomas. *The Gardener's Labyrinth*. Oxford University Press, 1987.

Hurst, Kim. *Herbs—The Secret Properties of 150 Plants*. University of Chicago Press, 2015.

Lawton, Barbara Perry. *Parsley, Fennel, and Queen Anne's Lace—Herbs and Ornamentals from the Umbel Family*. Timber Press, 2007.

Leyel, Mrs. C.F. *Herbal Delights: Tisanes, Syrups, Confections, Electuaries, Robs, Juleps, Vinegars and Conserves*. Richard Clay Ltd., 1987.

The National Society of the Colonial Dames of America. *Simples, Superstitions & Solace–Plant Material Used in Colonial Living.* Connecticut Printers Inc., 1970.

Peplow, Elizabeth. *The Herb Book–An A–Z of Useful Plants.* W.H. Allen & Co., 1984.

Plat, Sir Hugh. *Delightes for Ladies.* Crosby Lockwood & Son Ltd., 1948.

Romanné-James, C. *Herb Lore for Housewives.* Herbert Jenkins Ltd., 1938.

Simmons, Adelma G. *Herb Gardening in Five Seasons.* D. Van Nostrand Co. Inc., 1964.

These Blooming Herbs: A Book of Aromatic Gossip. E.P. Wilson Printers, 1940.

The Toilet of Flora. Herb Lovers Book Club, 1939.

von Bingen, Hildegard. *Hildegard's Healing Plants.* Translated by Bruce W. Hozenski. Beacon Press, 2001.

Karen O'Brien, owner of The Green Woman's Garden in Richmond, NH, is now investigating the possibilities of gardening in the woods as well as the fields. She has unusual herb plants for sale, including medicinal and native herbs, runs workshops on various herbal adventures, and occasionally participates at farmers markets and fairs. Karen lectures and presents workshops on all aspects of herbs and gardening. She is the Northeast District Membership Delegate of The Herb Society of America, served as Botany and Horticulture Chair and Development Chair of HSA, and past Chair of The New England Unit of HSA, was Secretary of the International Herb Association, and is Past President of the Greenleaf Garden Club of Milford. A Master Gardener, she is also the editor and contributing author to several IHA Herb of the Year™ books, including *Capsicum, Savory, Artemisia*, and *Elderberry*.

Parsley: Preserving the Harvest

Nancy Scarzello

A light misty rain is falling and after days and days of praying for relief from this drought, I can't resist finding myself out in it again and again. I've harvested just enough parsley for a pot of tea. Four of the largest outer stems come with me along with a couple of cilantro stalks going into flower. Kissed by the rain, the herbs and I are refreshed. Together we go for something new—parsley tea! I've never tried parsley tea, never even thought of it, yet I use parsley generously in my cooking for both the flavor and brightness it brings to so many dishes and for the myriad nutritional health benefits parsley offers.

But parsley tea? Something new for me.

The four stems yield about 1/4 cup of chopped parsley leaves to put into my French press along with 2 tablespoons of fresh cilantro, chopped, and a slice of lemon. Two cups of boiling water are then poured over the herbs and left to steep for 15 minutes. Strained, the liquid has just a hint of green and I expect the tea to be boring, uninteresting, and flavorless compared to the herbal teas I'm used to. Surprise! Full of the flavor and brightness it brings to my cooking, the tea is delightfully delicious! Having sipped this cup of tea just before lunch I can also attest to two of its medicinal qualities—a flavorful digestive and an effective diuretic. Now there are more ways to enjoy the harvest!

On my back porch, I have two Italian flat leaf parsley plants sharing a large clay pot with a couple of basils and a cherry tomato plant. I have two more in the veggie/herb/flower garden and find that four plants give me plenty of parsley even if I use it daily. So, when the frosts come in the autumn and the big harvest time is upon us, I want to preserve this emerald gem to brighten winter days. I've tried drying it several ways and though it may be crisp and colorful, I have never tasted dried parsley that retains the flavor beyond disappointing. Freezing, however, works beautifully.

Flat Leaf Parsley. *Diann Nance*

I harvest the parsley in the morning after the dew has dried, cutting the stems close to the base of the plant. I don't even wash it since I want the leaves dry for this method. (If I do need to wash it, I'll put the cut stems upright in a vase of water to air dry overnight, or wrapped in a paper towel in ziplock bags in the fridge.) Pull the tender leaves from the stems—I save the stems and put them in the freezer with other veggie scraps like carrot peels and celery tops. Just pop them into a ziplock and save for my next batch of soup stock— and fill a food processor with the leaves. Mine holds about 4 cups loosely packed leaves. Pulse several times until the parsley is chopped fine but still fluffy. You may have to stop and scrape down the sides a few times, but do not overdo it—you do not want a paste!

Now just put the chopped parsley (my 4 cups chop down to about 1 cup) into a zippered freezer bag, gently press out the air without compacting, and pop it in the freezer. I've done multiple batches on different days and just keep adding it to a gallon bag which usually gets just about full with my 4 plants. It stays fluffy when frozen and I can scoop out as much as I want without defrosting. This can be added to tomato sauce, soups, stews or any dish where it will be cooked (scampi!) or mixed into fresh, like dips, salads and dressings, smoothies and green drinks...and tea!

Another way to preserve parsley is in the old method of salt preserving. I tasted this amazing zesty condiment made by herbalist Caroline Gagnon last year and was inspired to give it a try. I used parsley in combination with other fresh herbs from the garden: rosemary, thyme, oregano, marjoram, and basil. Chop the herbs and place in a bowl to toss gently with salt. A ratio of 4:1, herbs to salt, is best. So, for every cup of chopped herbs, use 1/4 cup non-iodized salt. I use Diamond Crystal Kosher Salt—the flaky salt crystals layer beautifully. Once the herbs and salt are mixed together, loosely pack into a canning jar and store in the fridge. The herbs will settle some as the moisture is drawn out by the salt, but will be preserved close to their natural state.

Use as a seasoning or rub, remembering that it will be about 1/2 salt once it has settled. Adjust recipes as needed. The jar I made last summer looks and tastes the same a year later so I'll be making gifts to share from this season's harvest with the cooks in my circle of friends and family, parsley holding center stage.

Parsley dances in the wind. *Gail Wood Miller*

Nancy Scarzello is an herbalist with over 40 years experience as teacher, medicine-maker, grower and gardener. She lives in the Adirondacks of upstate New York where, to her delight, she can be found in the garden and among the wild ones of the forests, fields and waters near her home. Sharing her love of the natural world through teaching workshops and classes, making superior medicinal mushroom extracts and herbal products, writing about the natural world in her book, *Nature Through the Seasons*, and creating art, Nancy can be reached through email at forestbay@wcvt.com.

Japanese Wild Parsley Salad

Holly and Osamu Shimizu

Mitsuba (*Cryptotaenia japonica*), also known as Japanese wild parsley, is native to Japan and used widely as a seasoning and as a vegetable in a variety of Japanese food. All parts of the plant are edible but most often the young leaves and shoots are used, added toward the end of preparation since it turns bitter if cooked more than a few minutes. When I am in Japan, I see it in the markets and widely used on foods. I have made Chawanmushi (Japanese Steamed Egg Custard) and place the leaves on top before serving.

Other possibilities include use in soups, custards, vinegared foods, and seeds for seasoning. The refreshing flavor is a blend of parsley, chervil, and celery. It has many nutritional benefits including being high in potassium, calcium, vitamin C, carotene, and more. According to Osamu, who grew up in Japan but has not lived there for over 40 years, traditionally mitsuba is used with soup for the flavor, added on the top before serving to maintain fresh flavor. It is mixed with various salads like we would use "our" parsley.

A member of the carrot family (Apiaceae), mitsuba will grow well in partial shade. It is treated/grown like an annual even though it tends to behave like a biennial and sometimes like a short-lived perennial. I have grown it and treat it like an annual. Kitazawa Seed Co. is a good source for mitsuba seed.

The name *mitsuba* means "three leaves" in Japanese; the plants do have three evenly shaped, light green leaves that become darker green as they mature. Lovely star-shaped flowers reach around 3 feet when blooming and quickly turn to seed. For production, mitsuba is grown as an annual even though it is classified as a perennial. If allowed to go to seed, plants can come up generously so, if you don't want it to spread, cut back the seeds before they drop. The purple version (*Cryptotaenia japonica f. atropurpurea*) is grown as an ornamental plant in gardens although it can seed aggressively. The purple foliage becomes more pale in the summer and the plants have lovely pink umbels in summer.

This recipe for Japanese Summer Salad is refreshing and ideal for summer months.

Japanese Summer Salad

Makes 4 to 6 servings

1 large bowl of fresh lettuce
1 cucumber, thinly sliced
1 avocado, cut into small cubes
2 tablespoons roasted sesame seed
1/2 cup red onion, thinly sliced
1/2 cup shredded carrots
1 tablespoon chopped mitsuba

Salad Dressing

Juice of 1 lime, squeezed
1 tablespoon soy sauce
1 teaspoon brown sugar
1 teaspoon sesame oil
Freshly ground black pepper and salt to taste

Mix the greens and vegetables together in a large salad bowl.

In a separate glass bowl, whisk together lime juice, soy sauce, brown sugar, sesame oil, salt and pepper. Serve over salad. Refrigerate any leftover dressing.

Holly H. Shimizu is a nationally recognized horticulturist, consultant, and educator. With a rich background in all aspects of public gardens, extensive experience leading garden tours and workshops, and a proven commitment to plant conservation and sustainability, she has been making plants and gardens more accessible and exciting to both professionals and amateurs for over four decades. Find out more about Holly at www.hollyshimizu.com. **Osamu Shimizu** has worked in many gardens around the world, including Kew Royal Botanic Garden, and has designed gardens throughout Europe and the United States. He and Holly reside in Maryland.

Parsley's Distant Horizons

Skye Suter

Is parsley just an aside or an afterthought when it comes to our daily repast? This was the word and the wisdom for many of us whose youth spanned a few (okay, maybe more than a few) decades back. Curly parsley was the only parsley that existed in those days, at least in small town America where I grew up. A sprig of parsley could be found pressed into the top of a deviled egg or gracing a "fancy" plated dinner plate at home or in a restaurant. Other than that, it was pretty invisible. Today, new revelations about this wonderful little herb have expanded my parsley horizons.

My adulthood has seen the rise of flat leaf or Italian parsley almost to the exclusion of curly parsley. Although Italian parsley usurped curly parsley, the curly variety has been making a resurgence in recent years, and I'm glad to have it back in the game.

Italian parsley and curly parsley are considered the same, or different, depending on the source of opinion. Flavor compounds in Italian parsley give it the stronger flavor profile of the two, making it the preferred parsley in the kitchen. They can still be used interchangeably, keeping in mind the strength of one versus the other as it applies to a recipe. My opinion about the popularity of the flat leaf variety is that is also easier to manage under the kitchen knife. I also think it takes a bit more effort to release the flavor in curly parsley because of its chewier, tougher leaf texture. I find the flavor pretty consistent between both types and enjoy using either.

A few years ago I discovered parcel (*Apium graveolens* var. *secalinum*), an up and coming, chic substitute for parsley or celery. The herb is a cross between curly parsley and celery, hence the name. The taste is more like celery and is used in cooked form or raw in soups, stews, and salads. While parsley is a biennial where I live, parcel is perennial herb. I have grown parcel for four or five years in the same pot and have used it from time to time, but I still prefer my parsley.

Parcel (*Apium graveolens* var. *secalinum*) in bloom. *Skye Suter*

Besides holding sway in the culinary court, parsley can be employed as a natural dye and as a medicinal herb. Parsley is used to dye natural fabrics and yarns like cotton and wool. Around Easter, I dye eggs with natural dyes and like to use parsley leaves and stems to create a pretty yellow. To make color dyes for eggs, boil your natural ingredient of choice in a bit of water. Let it cool and remove the spent plant material. Use about one cup of your dye tea to about two tablespoons of white vinegar. Dip your eggs and get pretty colors.

Medicinal applications for parsley include help for bladder infections, kidney stones, constipation, asthma, and high blood pressure. Parsley helps to stimulate digestion as well as to improve it; it also increases menstrual flow and urine flow. Poultices or teas are applied externally for chapped or bruised skin, insect bites, and dark spots. Aerial and underground parts are used for medicine.

I have an interest in recipes and foods from different periods of time and different cultures. I get a big kick out of reading recipes or "receipts" from the past, whether from ancient Rome, Medieval Europe, or Colonial America. It is quite fun to compare outrageous ingredients and directions with our modern-day sensibilities. Old recipe books gave advice on how to cook and preserve foods but they have also scribed practical recipes for the home such as formulas to clean furniture or floors, medicinal solutions to take care of a sore throat or constipation, and self-care recipes for shampoo or toothpowder.

A Leaf from Parsley History

In ancient Rome and Greece, parsley was sometimes referred to as *stone celery*. The first Greek naturalists called parsley *petrosellinon*, which we find reflected in the modern botanical name *Petroselinum*. The botanical name for celery is *Apium graveolens* and the Roman name for celery was *apium*. Dioscorides listed parsley as a variety of celery and deemed it more valuable as healing herb rather than cooking herb. Historians find interchangeable and confusing name references to parsley and celery in the ancient world creating some difficulty in deciphering some writings and recipes. The English word "parsley" is derived from *petrosellinum*.

An ancient salad most often consisted of salted greens (lettuces) dipped in an oil and vinegar, or garum, the Roman's favorite fish condiment. (Think Worchestershire sauce.) Extra seasoning was added with a little bit of mint and parsley. A salad recipe from this time period included parsley along with other greens such as celery, cilantro, sorrel and of course lettuces.

Other recognizable herbs used during the time of the Roman Empire include *porrum*, leek, and *ligustrum*, lovage.

Roman gladiators applied parsley compresses before combat in the belief that it would redouble their courage and strength during their combat performance. This practice may have come from the use of parsley poultices for healing bruises and other superficial skin ailments. Crumbled, fresh leaves were also placed on wounds, burns, and sores to produce a cooling comfort.

At Roman banquets, the brows of participants were crowned with parsley to bring forth a gay and festive spirit and increase the appetite. In modern times, parsley has been used as an appetite stimulant, to promote digestion, for flatulence, and as a diuretic. The Romans certainly understood something of the qualities of parsley. During medieval times, parsley was used for flatulence, stomach aches, cough, and snake bite. Infusions of young leaves made a soothing eyewash and a concoction of the crushed seeds would take away freckles, as well as head and body lice.

Dutch settlers in New York brought herbs with them from the Old World. They introduced chives, marjoram, rosemary, tarragon, summer savory, tarragon, thyme, and parsley, with parsley being the most used of all. The 1776 American herb book, *An Herb Sallad for the Tavern Bowl* by Sidney Smith, features a recipe that included "all lettuces, sorrel, salad burnet, tarragon, lovage, shallots, garlic chives, chervil, watercress, and parsley."

Food

Parsley offers beneficial digestive qualities that make it a welcome accompaniment to kitchen options. Parsley is also pretty versatile and is used in many foods. Medieval housewives used it in salads, pottages, and teas. Parsley has nutritional value and was also a tonic for digestion made poor by a meager winter diet. Leafy greens offer therapeutic actions to ease indigestion, act as a digestive stimulant and a laxative, and a way to get vitamins and minerals.

Parsley finds its place in a range of dishes. It is often used within a recipe and then as garnish before serving. It can be the base of a pesto, added to a fresh salad, combined into fresh and cooked sauces, or added to baked goods. Parsley folded into ricotta is stuffed into pasta shells, put into lasagna, or added to the top of a pasta dish before serving. Parsley is found in familiar comfort foods like biscuits, parsley potatoes, or my favorite—dumplings boiled on top of a stew.

Beets and Parsley

I like expanding my parsley horizons through time and geography. The Middle East offers a multitude of fresh and cooked dishes that feature parsley. Recipes often combine ingredients such as tomatoes, cucumbers, grains (such as bulgur), and parsley in almost equal measures. Two of my recipes featuring beets follow this line of thinking with large measures of parsley.

Simple Beet Salad

I often enjoy a very simple and tasty salad featuring beetroot and parsley. It is nice as a side or as the main dish. Combine two or three cooled roasted beets which have been peeled and cut into bite-sized pieces, with a handful of minced parsley. Sprinkle salt and pepper to taste and dress with your favorite olive oil and balsamic vinegar. I sometimes add a few other minced herbs, fresh from the garden, but parsley is the main player.

Pink Beet Pasta

This pasta and beet dish was developed by Frambois Caterers of Staten Island. The addition of beets into this béchamel sauce makes it quite a colorful pasta dish. The resulting Pepto-Bismol color of the pasta sauce might even entice children to eat beets. However, I often gently fold in the beets at the end to get gentle swirls of color instead of a thoroughly solid pink. Chopped fresh herbs greatly enhance this dish, particularly parsley. I have also added basil and oregano. I normally use a substantial rigatoni but with children it is more fun to use bow-tie shaped pasta.

Serves 4 to 8

1 pound cooked pasta
2 tablespoons butter
2 1/2 tablespoons flour
1 1/2 cups whole milk, room temperature

Salt and freshly ground black pepper
1/2 cup + chopped parsley, parcel, chives, or a combination of your choice
2 to 4 tablespoons grated Parmesan cheese
2 to 3 medium sized beets, roasted, cooled, peeled, and cut into 1/2 cubes

Cook the pasta, drain, and set aside.

The béchamel sauce: Melt the butter in a heavy-bottom sauce pan at a low to medium heat. Add the flour, and stir for a couple of minutes to cook the flour/butter paste. Add the milk and continue to stir as the sauce thickens. This process takes 5 to 10 minutes. Start with a higher temperature, then after a few minutes, lower the heat as the sauce starts to thicken. When it comes to a creamy consistency, remove from the heat and add the salt, pepper, and chopped herbs. Add a couple of tablespoons of grated cheese into the sauce and more to taste.

Scrape and pour the sauce into the cooked pasta to combine. Put the pasta dressed with the béchamel into your serving dish. Gently fold in the beets and serve at the table.

Rethinking Old Recipes

Recipes from the past frequently called for exotic—for the time—spices like cinnamon or nutmeg, as well as lots of sugar. Spices and sugar were prohibitively expensive and limited to the kitchens of the ruling and wealthy merchant classes. These households could afford to record "receipts" that called for expensive and hard to find ingredients.

The lower classes had to purchase food goods at town markets when they could afford it, rely on foraged ingredients, or use ingredients they cultivated themselves. Luckily foraged herbs could be found near their homes to add flavoring to what could be a bland pottage or stew. During the Middle Ages, a *tansy* might have been served at an inn to all classes of pilgrim. A tansy was an omelette made mostly of eggs and chopped herbs. A *pottage* is a cooked meal made in a large cauldron or pot. The main ingredient is some type of grain and the word is often used synonymously with *porridge*.

An old recipe for pottage from the *English Housewife*, 1615.

The vegetable ingredients: *Violet leaves (petals), Succory (chicory), Strawberry leaves, Spinage (spinach), Langdebeef (a variety of bugloss), Marygold (Calendula) flowers, Scallions, and a little Parsley. This was added to oatmeal in the kettle to create a properly flavored pottage.*

Parsley in Italian is *Prezzemolo* which has some linguistic similarities with *Petroselinum*. Equating parsley with Italian dishes brings pesto to mind. Herb relishes and spreads are similar to pestos and are easily created to enhance a myriad of appetizers, baked goods, soups, and other goodies.

An herbal relish can be a topper for an appetizer toast, rustic bread, or deviled egg. Serve an herbal relish with a savory scone, a vegetable puff, or a savory pudding. Use herb combinations to complement your tastes and the items to be served. Use additional ingredients to suit your fancy such as other herbs or olives. The relish can be combined with a soft cheese such as a ricotta or mascarpone or drizzled over a vegetable soup. This recipe for an herbal relish is easily adapted to accommodate your culinary needs.

Herb Relish

1 packed cup of fresh Italian parsley
1/2 cup packed fresh mint, or basil
1/2 cup mixed herb leaves such as chives, marjoram, oregano,
          tarragon, and thyme
2 tablespoons white wine vinegar
5 to 6 large capers, or 4 to 5 pitted, Mediterranean style olives, optional
1/2 teaspoon salt
1/2 teaspoon fresh ground black pepper
1/2 cup extra virgin olive oil

Yields 1 1/2 to 2 cups

In a food processor, combine the herbs with the salt and vinegar. Pulse them a couple of times to combine, then drizzle olive oil into the machine while it is running on a low speed. Add more or less olive oil depending on how thin you want the Herb Relish. I prefer a thicker relish so it can be treated like a jelly or jam. If you want it thinner and more like a sauce, add more olive oil.

Refrigerate leftovers and use within two to three days.

Ye Olde Root Vegetable Puff

An old recipe for carrot or parsnip puffs from *The Compleat Housewife* by Eliza Smith.

Scrape and boil your carrots or parsnips tender; then scrape or mash them very fine, add to a pint of pulp the crumb of a penny-loaf grated, or some stale biscuit, if you have it, some eggs, but four whites, a nutmeg grated, some orange-flower-water, sugar to your taste, a little sack, and mix it up with thick cream. They must be fry'd in rendered suet, the liquor very hot when you put them in; put in a good spoonful in a place.

A Modern Root Vegetable Puff

Puffs and fritters are similar in that they are both bits of bite-sized fried goodness. Fritters are made with a flour batter while puffs rely on a vegetable mash mixed with bread crumbs. The puffs in this recipe can be made with a single root vegetable or a combination of several vegetables.

10 to 12 medium carrots, parsnips, or 6 to 8 medium potatoes
1 1/2 cups of panko or 1 cup of bread crumbs
2 large eggs, beaten
1 teaspoon freshly ground nutmeg or mace
1 pinch of cayenne, optional
3 tablespoons minced Italian parsley leaves
1 to 2 tablespoons finely minced parcel, celery, or lovage leaves
1/2 teaspoon salt
1/2 teaspoon freshly ground white pepper
2 tablespoons sherry, optional
1/2 cup heavy cream, milk, or half-and-half
Peanut oil or vegetable oil for frying

Scrape, peel, and clean the skin from the vegetables and cut them into large pieces. Boil carrots or parsnips for about 20 minutes and potatoes about 15 minutes, until tender. Drain the vegetables and mash smooth to create about 2 cups of pulp.

In a bowl combine the vegetable mash, panko, beaten eggs, nutmeg, cayenne, parsley, parcel, salt, pepper, sherry, and cream.

Preheat the frying oil to about 365° F in a large skillet. Pour enough oil in the pan to reach about halfway up the sides. Drop heaping tablespoons of the batter into the heated oil. Fry until each side is crispy and golden, about 1 to 2 minutes.

Drain on a rack over a plate, then serve hot or at room temperature. Serve with herb relish alone or a dollop of sour cream and herb relish.

Grow parsley in the garden for fun, flavor, and festivity. *Susan Belsinger*

References

Airy-Shaw, H. K. "The Correct Name of the Common Parsley." *Bulletin of Miscellaneous Information Royal Botanic Gardens*, Kew. DOI: 10.2307/4113472. https://www.jstor.org/stable/4113472?seq=1. Accessed 6/20/20.

Allen, Gary. *Herbs, A Global History. The Edible Series*. Reaktion Books Ltd, 2012.

Carew Hazlitt, William. *Old Cookery Books and Ancient Cuisine*. The Project Gutenberg eBook. Release Date: May 7, 2004. eBook #12293.

"Vitamins and Supplements, Parsley." *WebMD*. https://www.webmd.com/vitamins/ai/ingredientmono-792/parsley. Accessed 6/20/20.

Weinraub, Judith. *Salad, A Global History. The Edible Series*. Reaktion Books Ltd., 2016.

"What Is the Difference Between Flat-Leaf Parsley and Curly Parsley?" *Master Class*. https://www.masterclass.com/articles/what-is-the-difference-between-flat-leaf-parsley-and-curly-parsley#whats-the-difference-between-flatleaf-parsley-and-curly-parsley. Accessed 6/25/20.

Skye Suter broadcasts her fondness for art and plants through a number of disciplines. As a writer and illustrator, Skye contributes to the IHA's annual Herb of the Year ™ publication and other freelance projects. She also lectures on herbs and related subjects to interested groups, and teaches nature classes at a local nature center.

Currently, she pens plant-related articles, lectures on Zoom, and produces a series of newsletters and bulletins, including a monthly newsletter for the Staten Island Herb Society, a quarterly newsletter for the International Herb Association, and a tri-annual, seasonal bulletin for Friends of Blue Heron Park, Inc.

Visit Skye's website https://www.anherballeaf.com to view her publications, *An Herbal Leaf Journal* and *An Herbal Leaf Monthly Message*, which reflect an interest in plants, nature, art, crafting, cooking, and especially herbs. An archived section with selected copies of Monthly Messages and Journals is also available on the website as a subscription section. Skye can be reached at anherballeaf@gmail.com.

Parcel, or Amsterdam Celery. *Richter's Herbs.*

From *Richter's Herb 2020 Catalog*, Parcel or "Amsterdam Celery" (*Apium graveolens* var. *secalinum* 'Amsterdam'). A very nice leaf celery with finely cut, dark green glossy leaves. Use it like parsley and surprise your guests with its rich celery flavour and aroma. More compact than other leaf celeries, reaching only 25-50 cm (10-20") in height. S1677-100 Seeds: Pkt/$2.75, 10g/$7, 100g/$32.

Parsley Leaves. *Alicia Mann*

Healing Parsley

Flowering Parsley. *Susan Belsinger*

Sometimes

Shirley Russak Wachtel

Sometimes life needs parsley
When dejected by meat and bone
And the pretense of sweet cherry pie.
When the bread of the earth becomes
Too much to bear
And even milk straightforward and life-affirming
Is just not enough.

Sometimes life needs parsley
The curly kind
That's greener than green
Slick with cool water
Abundant and twisty
Spilling into gardens
Teasing at the edges of potato salad and split pea soup.

As impractical and tasteless
As sprinkles on a birthday cake
The seed-pecking goldfinch its only enemy
The world and its treasures, all a friend.
Look at its happy demeanor, touch and taste
This garnish for the soul.

Sometimes life needs parsley.

Shirley Russak Wachtel is an author and the host of a podcast called EXTRAordinary People which features inspiring people from all walks of life. Shirley is the recipient of the Middlesex County College 2017 Faculty Scholar Award, the author of several novels, and has written of a book of poetry, *In the Mellow Light*, along with several books for children, and a college-level remedial reading series, *Spotlight on Reading*. Her personal essays have been published in *The New York Times* OpEd section. Wachtel's short stories and poems have appeared in *Middlesex, biostories, River Poets Journal, Haiku Journal, emerge, Leaves of Ink, Whisper*, and other literary journals. In 2019, she was honored by the Center for Holocaust, Human Rights and Genocide Education for her acclaimed memoir, *My Mother's Shoes*, which follows her mother's journey during the Holocaust and as a new citizen in America, as well as her talks to students around the country. Shirley holds a Doctor of Letters Degree from Drew University. Learn more about Shirley's work at her website: https://www.shirleywachtel.com.

Soak a face mask in parsley tea to soothe and rejuvenate your skin. *Janice Cox*

Natural Beauty with Parsley

Janice Cox

Parsley is one of my favorite herbs to grow. I not only love using it in culinary recipes but it is one of my favorite ingredients when making my own natural beauty products. I love both the curly and flat leaf varieties and have them in pots on my Oregon patio where they grow almost year round. Having them nearby is a benefit, as I just need to step out my back door and clip off a few stems or a bunch depending on how much I need. I also plant them in my garden beds, as I like to have extra for drying and sharing with my friends. For an instant pick-me-up or a good digestive aid, nothing beats a fresh sprig of this bright green herb.

Drying parsley is super easy in the summer when it grows and spreads out in my yard here in Oregon. I made a simple drying tray out of some scrap wood and window screen that works really well. In the morning I clip off some leaves and lay them out on the tray. I then place it in a warm spot but not in direct sunlight and usually, by the end of the day, my leaves are dry.

You don't have to build a tray, as I have also dried leaves on plates and cookie sheets on my kitchen counter. Some people use their oven but I like the slow, old-fashioned air-dry method and I think it is a bit safer as I never burn my leaves. I then save them in glass jars and they are perfect for making teas, bath soaks, and facial toners. A good rule of thumb is to use half the amount of dry to fresh leaves. In other words, if a recipe calls for 1 cup of fresh leaves, you can use 1/2 cup dried leaves.

Parsley is probably best known as a breath or mouth freshener. We all remember being served a sprig on our dinner plate. It makes a nice green garnish but it is also useful for cleansing your mouth and settling your stomach after a heavy meal.

When it comes to body and skin care, parsley is a very valuable ingredient and can be used by all skin types. In fact, parsley is definitely trending and you will see it listed on the labels of anti-aging products. Parsley has become a key ingredient and is often listed by its botanical name *Petroselinum crispum* on product labels.

Parsley is an excellent source of vitamin C, which is important for healthy skin. Eating parsley and sipping parsley tea or juice is a good way to improve the appearance of your skin. Parsley is also rich in vitamin A, the beauty vitamin, which helps in maintaining collagen and healing. You will see many anti-aging products featuring parsley and parsley seed oil for this reason. Parsley seed oil is difficult to create at home with common kitchen equipment but you can make your own infused oil using a light oil such as almond or jojoba oil with dried parsley leaves. When making infused oils, you never want to use fresh plant material, only dried. Fresh leaves contain moisture that can cause bacteria to grow in your products.

Another useful beauty ingredient is parsley juice or tea. When parsley juice is used in under-eye compresses or sheet masks, it is soothing and acts as an anti-inflammatory ingredient. If you have under-eye puffiness or dark circles, this infusion will help soothe and calm your skin. Create a simple and soothing facial mask by mixing together plain sour cream or yogurt with some fresh, chopped green parsley leaves. This same mixture also works well to calm sunburned or itchy skin conditions.

Parsley, like many herbs, also has anti-bacterial properties, helpful in treating troubled skin or acne breakouts. You can make a simple strong tea using fresh or dried parsley leaves to use after washing your face. Simply spray or dab the parsley tea with a clean cotton pad onto clean skin but do not rinse.

You can also combine parsley with green tea, which is effective in treating troubled skin conditions. I must note that, if using parsley on your skin is new, you will want to do a patch test first. This is true with any new product that you want to use. Simply rub a bit inside your arm or behind your leg and wait a few hours to see if your skin reacts to the new ingredient.

Parsley is good for your hair and some people believe that it can prevent hair loss. I think this is because it is naturally cleansing to your scalp and a clean, healthy scalp will produce healthy hair. Create a simple hair rinse to use after shampooing by mixing some parsley, a tablespoon of apple cider vinegar, and a cup of water. It is important to note that you never want to use vinegar directly on your skin or hair. Always dilute it first in water. This cleansing rinse will not only keep your hair clean, but it will also keep your scalp healthy and remove any dandruff or surface impurities.

Here are a few of my favorite natural beauty recipes that you can create at home using parsley. If you do not have it growing in your yard, not to worry.

This herb is so popular you will easily find it in the produce section of every grocery store. If you are looking for dried leaves, they too are there in the spice section. Enjoy!

Parsley Skin Freshener

We all know that parsley is a powerful mouth freshener, but it also makes a mild and gentle toner for the skin. Use this freshener throughout the day to keep your complexion clean and radiant. Parsley is easy to find in any grocery store or farmers market. It's also a snap to grow in your garden or in a container. Parsley especially loves to be planted next to roses. It is believed that planting parsley at the base of your rose bush makes the flowers smell sweeter.

Yield: 8 ounces

1/2 cup chopped fresh parsley
1 cup boiling water

Place the parsley in a ceramic bowl and pour the boiling water over the leaves. Allow the mixture to cool completely, then strain and pour into a clean container.

To use: Apply to your skin using a clean cotton ball or small spray bottle. Use this tea in the recipe below.

Parsley Sheet Mask

Sheet masks have become so popular, they are sold almost everywhere. The purpose of these types of masks is to treat and hydrate your skin. They allow you to apply solutions to your skin such as herbal teas, aloe vera gel, and floral waters. The fabric keeps the mixture next to your skin without evaporating or running off. They are also simple to make yourself at home and, if you repurpose a piece of natural fabric, you can make one by tracing your face and cutting out eye, nose, and mouth holes. These fabric masks can be used over and over and are a great way to repurpose fabric. You can also purchase mask sheets online or at beauty supply stores.

This recipe features parsley tea, which is perfect for all skin types. You can make up several masks and keep in a jar inside your refrigerator. These cool masks are especially refreshing after working out or on a hot summer day.

Yield: 4 ounces

1/2 cup strong parsley tea, cooled (see previous recipe)
1 teaspoon raw honey
1 tablespoon aloe vera gel

Stir together all ingredients. Soak a cotton mask in the solution for a minute or two. (You can also store in the refrigerator for later use. It should last a day or two.)

To use: Wring out your mask and place on clean skin. Relax and lie down with your mask in place. Let sit 10 to 15 minutes. Remove and rinse skin and pat dry.

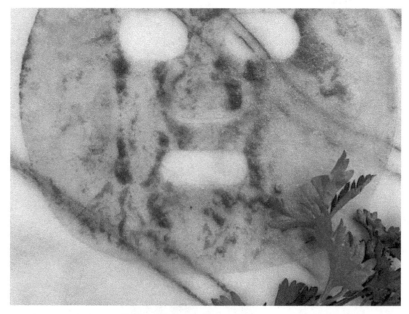

Parsley Sheet Mask. *Janice Cox*

Calming Parsley Facial Mask

Finely chopped parsley is soothing to blotchy or troubled complexions. To deep cleanse and freshen normal-to-dry skin, combine parsley, sour cream, and egg whites or aloe vera gel. This mixture will calm and cleanse your skin and can be used weekly to keep your skin clean and clear. For oily skin types, you can add 1 teaspoon fresh lemon juice.

Yield: 2 ounces

2 tablespoons fresh parsley, chopped, or 1 tablespoon dried parsley leaves
2 tablespoons sour cream or plain yogurt
1 egg white or 1 tablespoon aloe vera gel

Combine all ingredients and spread onto clean skin. Let sit for 20 minutes, then rinse with warm water followed by a splash of cool water. Pat your skin dry and use your favorite moisturizer or natural oil.

Ingredients for a Calming Parsley Facial Mask. *Janice Cox*

Herbal Shampoo

You can create your own herbal shampoo using a single herb or a combination of your favorite herbs. This recipe uses parsley, mint, and rosemary. All work well to keep your scalp healthy and clean. Making your own shampoo is easy but also may take a bit of getting used to after using commercial brands. Homemade shampoos do not contain some of the detergents that can create that head-full-of-suds feeling. This recipe uses castile soap that is much easier on your hair and scalp.

Yield: 8 ounces

1 tablespoon dried parsley
2 teaspoons dried mint
1 teaspoon dried rosemary
1/2 cup boiling water
1/2 cup mild liquid soap such as castile soap

Place all of the herbs in a glass bowl and pour the boiling water over them. Let the mixture steep for at least 20 minutes until cool, then strain out all solids. Stir in the liquid soap and pour the mixture into a clean container with a tight fitting lid. Let sit overnight and the shampoo will thicken.

To use: Pour a small amount into your hand and massage into your scalp and hair. Rinse well.

Stimulating Scalp Toner

This toner keeps the scalp healthy and clean. It contains fresh mint and parsley, both of which are naturally astringent and refreshing. You can also use it throughout the day to keep your scalp clean and happy. Fill a small spray bottle with this recipe and spritz the toner onto your hair and scalp for a quick, refreshing pick-me-up. It should last a week or two depending on how it is handled; for a longer shelf life store in the refrigerator.

Yield: 8 ounces

1/4 cup fresh mint leaves, chopped

1/4 cup fresh parsley leaves, chopped
1/2 cup boiling water
1/2 cup witch hazel
2 tablespoons vodka

Place the fresh mint and parsley leaves inside a glass or ceramic container and pour the boiling water over them. Let this mixture cool completely, then strain out the leaves by pouring through a coffee filter or fine strainer. Mix together the parsley-mint water with the witch hazel and vodka. Stir well. Pour the refreshing mixture into a clean bottle with a tight-fitting lid.

To use: Pour a small amount onto a clean cotton ball or pad and rub over your scalp. You may also massage it lightly into your scalp with your fingertips.

Parsley Mouth Rinse

Parsley leaves freshen the breath and clean and disinfect the gums. This rinse has a bright, green flavor and can be used throughout the day to keep your mouth healthy. Like many natural products, this one also has multiple uses so it is perfect for travel or if you want to limit products on your shelves. It also makes a nice after-bath splash and facial toner. Because it contains fresh parsley, and depending upon how often you use this product, you may want to store it in the refrigerator to extend its shelf life.

Yield: 8 ounces

2 tablespoons fresh parsley leaves or 1 tablespoon dried
1 cup boiling water
2 tablespoons rosewater

Place the parsley leaves in a glass or ceramic dish and pour the boiling water over them. Let this mixture steep for several hours, then strain and discard the leaves. Add the rosewater and stir well. Pour into a clean container.

To use: Pour a small amount into a clean glass and rinse your mouth after brushing your teeth and gums. Swish the liquid back and forth in your mouth and gargle with it.

Pretty Parsley. *Janice Cox*

To complement your "at home spa" experience, you can serve refreshing drinks infused with parsley. This basic simple syrup recipe featuring fresh parsley is perfect for adding to teas, smoothies, and cocktails. I like to use curly parsley but any favorite variety will work. I mix it with fresh cucumber juice and lime juice over ice for a refreshing summer drink. You can even add a little vodka or gin for a garden cocktail.

Yield: 8 ounces

1 cup fresh parsley
1 cup water
1 cup sugar

Place all ingredients in a saucepan and bring to a boil. Turn off heat and stir well until all of the sugar is dissolved. Let steep for 30 minutes then strain out the parsley leaves and pour into a clean container. Store in the refrigerator. It should last for a two to three weeks; you can also freeze it for year-round use.

Janice Cox is an expert on the topic of natural beauty and making your own body care products using simple kitchen and garden ingredients. She is the author of five books on the topic: *Natural Beauty at Home, Natural Beauty for All Seasons, Natural Beauty from the Garden, Beautiful Luffa,* and *Beautiful Lavender.* She is the beauty editor for *Herb Quarterly Magazine* and a member of the Mother Earth Living Magazine advisory board. She lives in Medford, Oregon, where she loves to grow herbs and flowers. For more information you can visit her website at www.JaniceCox.com.

The chlorophyll-rich leaves of parsley are full of vitamins and minerals.
Susan Belsinger

Parsley's History of Medicinal Uses

Davy Dabney

Most of us are familiar with the culinary uses for parsley. But did you know parsley has an extensive history of medicinal uses? Throughout ancient times, parsley was used as an herbal cure. In fact, it was not until the Middle Ages that parsley started being used for culinary purposes.

In ancient Greek mythology, superstition and belief in the gods guided the medical perception on recovering from infections and illness. The Romans had a more down to earth approach on curing illness, using trial and error techniques to find different ways to fight diseases. Long before the Roman Empire, people were driven to find ways to fight plagues that periodically struck. Plants were used as cures and as aids to improve health, or at least, to make people feel more comfortable. Egyptian scrolls discovered in the pyramids record that, as early as 1700 BC, garlic, rosemary, hemp, and parsley were used for health as well as preserving bodies for burial.

By the first century BC, many cultures had begun keeping records of their healing remedies. From 200 BC to about 1400 AD, many educated and adventurous people traveled extensively through parts of Europe and the Mediterranean areas to share information and views on the causes and cures of various diseases. A few even ventured as far as Asia. An early Chinese herbal, apparently written during the first century BC, was among one of the earliest records of treatments and cures. During this same period, India and other cultures were also collecting and recording their successes and failures using plants for medicinal uses.

As early as 2000 BC, Egyptian physicians were using their knowledge of anatomy to guide their use of plants to maintain good health. They used parsley as a diuretic, and mixed it with other herbs such as dill and juniper to sooth stomach problems. Because of their knowledge of anatomy from preserving bodies, the Egyptian physicians were thought by many other physicians to be the most advanced in the world.

Around 430 BC, Thucydides, an ancient Greek historian, hypothesized that exposure to infection, if the patient survived, helped build immunity toward being re-infected. He used a strong parsley tea to help those who survived. Other ancient medical practitioners also recognized the healing properties of parsley. Even in 980 BC, Avicenna, a Persian doctor used poultices made of parsley along with basil and juniper to treat injuries sustained by soldiers during battle. Puntus, a Roman anatomist in the second century BC, used parley tea to ease stomach distress, regulate menstrual flow, and treat colic in babies. During the same era, Greek healer and poet Nicander gave parsley to his chickens to help them lay more eggs. Apuleius, a second century AD Roman philosopher and scholar, credited Sardinian parsley with similar curative powers.

One of the most well-known physicians (circa 150 AD) was the Greek Claudius Galen, who after studying herbal medicine and treating hundreds of wounded gladiators with botanical remedies, became the personal physician of Roman Emperor Marcus. He prescribed a strong decoction of parsley root for falling sickness (epilepsy) and used parsley seed tea to sooth the liver and spleen. He also used the parsley seed infusion to try to battle the plague, albeit unsuccessfully.

Many Roman physicians laid parsley leaves on inflamed eyes and parsley juice added to wine was dropped in ears to ease earache. The Romans copied Egyptian techniques to distill and extract the juice of leaves, seeds, stems, and roots for easier use. They used all parts of parsley to break up kidney stones; to alleviate insect bites, painful digestion, anemia, and hypertension; and to inhibit tumor growth as well as many other illnesses. In addition, they used parsley to stop the flow of breast milk, induce abortions, regulate menstrual flow, and as an expectorant. A salve made with parsley seed was used to stimulate hair growth. It was thought that adding parsley to food would help it stay fresh longer. Other uses were to treat dysentery, gallstones, anemia, pains of the liver, heart and blood circulation, to expel parasites, and as a wash to remove lice, stop itching, and clear up bruises .

Pedanius Dioscorides, circa 40-90 AD, the Greek pharmacologist who wrote *De Materia Medica*, the reference book used for more than 200 years, recorded these and many other uses for parsley. Throughout history many women, housewives as well as nuns, were involved in finding cures and used parsley to help with a multitude of ailments. For example, Hildegard of Bingen, a German herbalist and Benedictine abbess, used parsley boiled in wine to relieve heart and chest pains, and compresses of parsley leaves to ease painful arthritic stiffness. Many cultures have continued to use these treatments and remedies with many good results.

Today, we understand why parsley is such a valuable health aide. Recent studies have shown that parsley contains vitamins, minerals, and antioxidants that help prevent cellular damage from free radicals—carotenoids, flavonoids, vitamins A, B folate and C, K, apigenin, and myristicin. Studies show that diets which include these help lower the risk of type 2 diabetes, colon cancer, and heart disease. Parsley also contains beta carotene, lutein and zeaxanthin which help to protect eyes and may be prescribed as supplements to prevent macular degeneration.

According to the British Pharmacopeia, distilling an extract of crushed, fresh parsley seeds can produce liquid apiol, or green oil of parsley. This oleoresin was first made by two doctors from Brittany in 1849, who used it to suppress a plague during that time. It has also been used to treat malaria. Dosage is important with any medicine or substance. According to Wikipedia, "Apiol is an irritant and, in high doses, it can cause liver and kidney damage. Cases of death due to attempted abortion using apiol have been reported."

It is heartening to know that our ancestors were more intelligent and resourceful than most people realize. Perhaps it may help us to refocus on their discoveries and incorporate them into our appreciation that many of their remedies worked. My hope is that our educational agenda may quit focusing on war and instead put more emphasis on things that have given us benefits and inspire interest in our current lives such as art, music, nature. In doing so, we could possibly encourage more people to have feelings of empathy and respect for all living creatures.

References

"Apiol." *Wikipedia*. Https://en.wikipedia.org/wiki/Apiol. Accessed 6/30/20.

Baker, H.G. *Plants and Civilization*. Wadsworth Publishing Co. London, 1970.

Buck, Albert H. *The Growth of Medicine*. Yale University Press, 1917.

Bailey, L.H. *Manual of Cultivated Plants*. Macmillian Publishers, 1968.

Grieve, Maude. *A Modern Herbal*. Dover Publishing, 1971 (1931).

Parkinson, John. *Garden of Pleasant Flowers*. Dover Publications, 1976 (1656).

North, Michael. "The History of Herbs." *The Herbarist*. Herb Society of America,1998. 41-43.

Davy Dabney, a founding member of the IHA (originally known as IHGMA, the International Herb Growers and Marketers Association), has been a business owner, an instructor, and mentor in the world of herbs and plants. She is a Life Member of the Herb Society of America, member of the Kentucky Herb Business Association, and owner of Dabney Herbs. With the help of the Wednesday Weeders, she planted and tended a superior herb garden at Farmington Historic Home in Kentucky. From 2003 to 2016, she was Superintendent of the Plant and Flower Department of the Kentucky State Fair, overseeing displays of over 3000 entries including plants and arrangements. She loves learning about exciting new plants, consulting and writing, and occasionally sitting on her deck with friends, enjoying the beauty of nature, and letting someone else do the weeding!

The Medicinal Properties
of Parsley

Daniel Gagnon, Medical Herbalist

Parsley (*Petroselinum crispum*) [Apiaceae] (McGuffin 2000)

Other common names
French: Persil
German: Petersilie
Italian: Prezzemolo
Spanish: Perejil
Russian: Petrushka
United Kingdom: Garden parsley, common parsley, rock parsley
(Nickell 1976)
Indian: Bilati (Bartram 1998)

Former Latin names
Apium crispum, Apium petroselinum, Carum petroselinum, Petroselinum hortense, Petroselinum sativum, Petroselinum vulgare (Duke 1985).
Petroselinum comes from the Greek, *petros* – stone, and *selinon* – wild celery (Fournier 1948)

Part Used: Leaf, root, seed, essential oil (Uphof 1968)

Parsley and its Origin

Many herbal authors suggest parsley is native to the Eastern Mediterranean (Wren 1988). Other authors, including the botanist Linnaeus, point toward Sardinia, while still others (De Candolle) state the herb is a native of Turkey, Algeria, and Lebanon. It has been imported and grown in many Northern hemisphere countries of the world. Since its introduction into Britain in the sixteenth century, it has naturalized in various parts of England and Scotland, where it can be found on old walls and rocks (Grieve 1971).

Second-year 'Italian Giant' going to seed. *Pat Kenny*

It is generally thought that parsley leaves were used to braid crowns for the winners of the Nemean games in ancient Greece. The athletic and musical competitions were held in July in honor of Zeus at the Temple of Zeus at Nemea in Argolis, the southeastern region of Greece. These games occurred biennially in the same years as the Isthmian games held in the Isthmus of Corynth (Leclerc 1976). However, there is ongoing controversy among academics as to whether the braided crowns were made from parsley or wild celery (*Apium graveolens*) leaves (Encyclopedia Britannica 2020, Rodriguez 2020).

The two main varieties grown for their leaves are divided into plain leaf and curly leaf. Other varieties include extra double curled, moss curled, and curled dwarf. In Europe, turnip-rooted parsley produces large roots that are eaten when cooked (Uphof 1968).

Parsley as Food

Parsley is known as a healthful garnish. However, make parsley more than a beautiful garnish and eat it to get the health benefits described below. The leaves and roots, fresh or dried, are served as vegetables or condiments. In Europe, parsley is often used in egg, fish, fowl, meat, shellfish, and soup dishes. In France, it has maintained a ubiquitous presence for centuries. For example, a mixture of finely chopped parsley and shallot is added as a *persillade* toward the end of cooking a dish. It is also important in *bouquet garni*, in butters and vinegars, in *vinaigrette*, as well as in sauces *ravigote*, *tartare*, and *verte*. In the Middle East, tabbouleh made with finely chopped parsley is a culturally important dish. The minced parsley is mixed with mint, onion, and chopped tomatoes, as well as bulgur, and seasoned with olive oil, lemon juice, salt, and bell pepper (Duke 1985).

The top five states producing parsley leaf as a food in the United States are California, New Jersey, Texas, Florida, and Hawaii, with California producing over 40 percent of the parsley leaf sold in American supermarkets (Western Institute for Food Safety and Security 2016).

A Short Herbal Medicine History of Parsley

Parsley has been used for its medicinal properties for centuries. Hippocrates (460-370 BCE) is known as the father of Western medicine. He wrote about parsley as an herb capable of causing an abortion. Greek native, Theophrastus (371 to 287 BCE) is considered the father of botany. He advocated parsley to fight painful or difficult urination and to get rid of kidney stones. Both Pliny the Elder (23 to 79 AD), a naturalist, and Dioscorides (40 to 90 AD), a Greek physician, used parsley seeds and roots to favor the elimination of urine and to induce menstruation. Another Greek physician named Galen (129 to 210 AD) advocated the use of parsley for water retention. He also suggested it for disorders of the womb and bladder (Leclerc 1976).

Ibn Rushd (1126 to 1198 AD), known in the Western world as Averroes, was a Muslim Andalusian who prescribed the use of parsley to induce copious urination. Some historians report that the Romans would give parsley to gladiators before fights as the plant was reputed to give strength, reflex, and cunning (Mésségué 1975). Constantine the African, who died around 1098 AD, was a North African Muslim who converted to Christianity, moved to Italy, and translated many books of the great masters of Arabic medicine into Latin. His books were used as textbooks for physicians from the Middle Ages to the seventeenth centuries. He suggested parsley for renal abscesses and bladder problems (Leclerc 1976).

More recently, Henri Leclerc, a French physician who coined the word *phytotherapy* in 1913, advocated for the use of fresh parsley root to induce the production and elimination of urine (Leclerc 1976).

Parsley's Constituents

The chemical composition of herbs is often of interest to individuals who want to gain a better understanding of how herbal constituents may influence the function of the human body. The following are some of the known constituents found in parsley.

The fresh parsley leaf contains appreciable amounts of vitamins A (as beta-carotene), B (including folic acid and B6), C, E, and K as well as bioflavonoids. The leaf is also a rich source of dietary fiber and minerals including calcium, copper, iron, magnesium, manganese, potassium, silica, and sulfur (Kirschmann 1996, Bartram 1998).

The nutritional benefits from parsley are easily accessed when eating fresh parsley leaves in foods such as tabbouleh. One ounce (30 g) of fresh parsley, an amount easily ingested in a tabbouleh serving, provides 72 mg of vitamin C, the minimum daily intake of this essential nutrient required to prevent deficiency symptoms. In the same serving of tabbouleh, parsley leaf delivers four times the amount of vitamin A needed by the human body on a daily basis.

Parsley leaves are rich in fibers and minerals, important dietary factors that help maintain health. Dietary fibers are essential for intestinal regularity as well as to maintain healthy cholesterol and blood sugar levels. Potassium is an important component of cells and body fluids that help regulate heart rate and blood pressure. Iron is essential for healthy red blood cell production. Manganese is used by the body as a co-factor to manufacture a powerful antioxidant enzyme, *superoxide dismutase*. The other minerals found in parsley help to strengthen hair, nails, and skin. A full serving of foods rich in fresh parsley leaves, such as tabbouleh, provides the necessary amounts of the nutrients described above. But keep in mind that very small amounts of dried leaf used sparingly in cooking offer negligible amounts of nutrients to the diet.

Parsley leaf water extract, as found in a cup of parsley tea, provides bioflavonoids, such as apigenin, luteolin, quercetin, and kampferol. These bioflavonoids have been shown to possess substantial antihistaminic properties which help to reduce the severity of allergies (Duke 1985).

Parsley herb also contains small amounts of volatile oil (0.05% to 0.3%), furocoumarins, consisting mostly of bergapten (up to 0.02%), with smaller amounts of xanthotoxin and isopimpinellin, flavonoids (apiin, luteolin-7-diglucoside, luteolin-7apiolglucoside, apigenin 7-glucoside, and luteolin-7-diglucoside and others), 2-22% proteins, 4% fat, sugars, and others (Duke 1985, Leung 1996).

Parsley seed contains a considerable amount of volatile oil (2-7%), 13 to 22% fixed oil consisting mainly of petroselinic acid (up to 70%), with small amounts of palmitic, myristic, stearic, oleic, linoleic, and myristolic acids. It also contains flavonoids, apiin, and traces of bergapten (Duke 1985).

The Indications of Parsley in Herbal Medicine

Parsley has been used in herbal medicine for thousands of years. The most common indications for this plant include water retention, edema, cystitis, gravel, kidney inflammation, painful urination, and renal abscesses. Women have long used parsley for the absence of menstruation, delayed menstruation, painful menstruation, leucorrhea, and PMS. Parsley has the ability to stimulate the uterus and promote delayed menstruation. It is used against digestive troubles, dyspepsia, swelling or engorgement of internal organs, gallbladder weakness, gallstones and jaundice as well as liver and spleen diseases. The root and the entire plant are used in decoctions against circulatory weaknesses, hemorrhoids, and diverse skin afflictions. It has been recommended for respiratory issues such as dyspnea (difficulty or

This row of healthy and thriving, second-year parsley plants is beginning to bloom in the vegetable garden. *Susan Belsinger*

labored breathing), persistent coughs, and in humid asthma (Leclerc 1976, Ellingwood 1983, Kirschmann 1996).

Parsley is used for allergies, asthma, itching of the skin and scalp, eczema, and other allergic manifestations (Duke 1985, Menzies-Trull 2003). Even though it has long been used as a laxative, parsley leaf tea was once served in the trenches during the First World War to troops suffering from dysentery (Duke 1985). The seed has traditionally been used as an abortifacient (Leung 1996).

Parsley seed works primarily on the kidneys and urogenital organs, strongly moves stagnation, and clears spasms and infections. (Holmes 1989). Parsley leaf is also an excellent breath freshener when chewed and is especially useful to eliminate garlic and onion breath (Duke 1997).

Parsley's Herbal Actions

The plant offers anti-allergic, aperitive (increases gastric juice secretion), aquaretic (a diuretic that doesn't deplete the body's mineral levels), anti-inflammatory, antimicrobial, antioxidant, antirheumatic, antispasmodic, carminative (expels gas from the digestive system), emmenagogue (starts or stimulates the menstrual flow), expectorant (increases the expulsion of mucus from the respiratory system), febrifuge (reduces fevers), gastric tonic, hypotensive (reduces blood pressure), and laxative properties. Parsley is also a mild brain tonic, mild sudorific (increases sweating), and offers uterine tonic properties. In addition, it is a mild adrenal and thyroid gland activator (Fournier 1948, Leung 1996, Bartram 1998, Stansbury 2018).

Parsley seed actions are quite different from the action of the root or the leaf and offer stimulant, antispasmodic, and antiseptic properties (Holmes 1989).

The Medicinal Proprieties of Parsley

Parsley has significant medicinal properties and offers substantial health benefits. Here are eight major medicinal areas where parsley can be of use to achieve and maintain human health.

Parsley and the Urinary System

Parsley is best known for its effects on the human urinary system. Practitioners of herbal medicine use parsley leaf and root in renal congestion, inflammation of the kidneys and bladder (nephritis, cystitis, and urethritis), renal abscesses, as well as for urinary stones and urine retention. It is a specific for urinary pain, burning and tingling, perineal pain and sensation, and "voluptuous" itching of genitals. It has been used for anuria (failure of the kidneys to produce urine) which may be associated with renal failure and/or heavy metal toxicity (Stanbury 2018). An infusion of parsley leaf is beneficial when urination is painful, and irritating to mucous membranes, such as in cases of nephritis. It is also useful in bladder inflammation especially when there is a scalding sensation of the urinary passages during urination. One of the advantages of using parsley leaf infusion during an acute urinary tract infection is that it will not create additional inflammation. Not all diuretics work that way; some are contraindicated during acute urinary tract inflammation as they can produce more inflammation (Ellingwood 1983). The root has been used effectively to relieve edema from poor blood circulation (Felter 1983).

There are many herbs that may be used for painful urination (dysuria). Parsley herb or root is often used with other urinary tract specific plants such as buchu (*Agathosma betulina*) leaf, burdock (*Arctium lappa*) seed, cornsilk (*Zea mays*), silky flower thread, couchgrass (*Agropyron repens*) root, dandelion (*Taraxacum officinale*) leaf, goldenrod (*Solidago canadensis*) herb, gravel root (*Eupatorium purpureum*) root, and marshmallow (*Althea officinalis*) root (Stansbury 2018). Make a tea from any of these and drink as much as 3 cupfuls per day.

Parsley's diuretic activity is seemingly due to constituents called apiole and flavones. These constituents stimulate the urinary system, specifically the functional part of the kidneys called the renal parenchyma (Van Hellemont 1986). Many of the Apiaceae family members also have the effect of relaxing urinary smooth muscles. Herbs with these properties include celery (*Apium graveolens*), parsley, and fennel (*Foeniculum vulgare*). They are often featured in folkloric formulations for renal pain, hypertension, and bronchospasm due to muscle-relaxing effects on the urinary, vascular and respiratory muscle fibers (Stansbury 2018).

Keep in mind that the leaf and root are less active than the fruit (seed). The fruit possesses an energetic diuretic action. Excellent results are obtained with seed infusion even in total anuria (situations where the kidneys do not produce urine, for example, in mercury intoxication cases) (Van Hellemont 1986).

Parsley Leaf, Female Health, Breast Pain, and Breast-feeding

Parsley has been a friend for centuries. It has been used for amenorrhea (the absence of menstruation), delayed menstruation, painful menstruation, leukorrhea (thick, whitish or yellowish vaginal discharge often due to an estrogen imbalance), and PMS. It has the ability to stimulate the uterus and promote delayed menstruation. For painful menstruation, it is often combined with other herbs such as buchu (*Agathosma betulina*) leaf, black haw (*Viburnum prunifolium*), and cramp bark (*Viburnum opulus*). Parsley leaf has also been used for premenstrual tension (PMT) and menopausal hot flushes. Drink up to 3 cupfuls per day (Hutchens 1973).

The medical term for breast pain is mastalgia. There are two main types of mastalgia. The first type is called cyclical mastalgia and is a recurring pain that is most often linked to the menstrual cycle. It is almost always hormonal in nature. The second type is called non-cyclical mastalgia and the pain may come from the breast itself or from the nearby muscle or joint and is felt in the breast. Breast pain can range from merely being bothersome to excruciating and can be treated effectively using a parsley leaf anti-inflammatory poultice as a first-line treatment. This treatment is most beneficial in cases where the cause of the pain is not yet obvious and symptomatic relief is needed. Perhaps the best part of this treatment is that a parsley leaf poultice carries no risk of adverse effects (Yarnell 2003).

Cyclical breast disorders are often caused by a number of interrelated hormonal factors which can lead to breast pain, swelling, and breast tissue changes. An herb called chaste tree (*Vitex agnus-castus*) berries taken internally is an excellent addition to parsley leaf poultices to resolve the issue. The benefits of this herb are achieved by taking 40 drops of the extract daily over a period of three to nine months. Long-term administration of chaste tree is sometimes necessary to maintain the benefits of this herb. Positive changes to the menstrual cycle are usually seen within the first month. However, some women report longer or shorter menstrual cycles than usual at the beginning of treatment until hormonal balance is achieved (Trickey 1998).

Mashed and unheated parsley leaves were once applied to the breasts of nursing mothers to stop the flow of milk when they were done with breast feeding (Bartram 1998). Additionally, taking a tea made from sage (*Salvia officinalis*) leaves assisted in the drying up of breast milk production (Nissim 1986).

Prior to the advent of antibiotics, herbal medicine treatment often saved patients' lives. Dr. Henri Leclerc reports in his book *Précis de phytothérapie* (1929) about a doctor who consulted with a woman suffering from anuria as a consequence of puerperal fever, an often fatal postpartum infection. In the days prior to antibiotics, women commonly died from such an infection, leaving helpless children without mothers. However, in this case, the patient was restored to health by using a strong decoction of fresh parsley root (100 grams per kilogram of water). Within a few days, the patient experienced an abundant diuresis, the fever completely dissipated, and she was quickly restored to health.

Parsley and Digestive Issues

In Europe, aperitive roots have been used to improve digestive health. They help to restore the appetite, stimulate the secretion of gastric juices, increase the flow of bile, revitalize the production of pancreatic enzymes and other digestive fluids, and open up the bowel. Parsley root is one of the five major aperitive roots. The others include fennel (*Foeniculum vulgare*) root, butcher's broom (*Ruscus aculeatus*) root, wild celery (*Apium graveolens*) root, and asparagus (*Asparagus officinalis*) root. These five roots, individually or collectively, are reputed to help individuals who are anemic, listless, or convalescent as well as those who lack energy and need a spring in their step. They are highly recommended against liver issues, jaundice, eczema, cellulitis, rheumatism, gout, flatulence, and poor digestion (Mésségué 1975).

Parsley leaf plays an important role in the prevention and/or treatment of duodenal or gastric ulcers. Modern science has shown that oxidative stress plays a key role in stress-induced gastric injury. A recent study investigated the effect of fresh parsley leaf on gastric damage from duodenal or gastric ulcers. The study was inspired by, and based on, the experience of one of the authors whose gastric burning and pain induced by stress were relieved shortly after eating fresh parsley. A healthy mucus layer covering the surface of the stomach and intestinal tract is an important protective layer against injuries that lead to ulcers. The researcher showed that adding parsley leaf to the diet was effective in reducing stress-induced gastric injury by supporting the body's cellular antioxidant defense system. Parsley is well known to contain high levels of powerful antioxidants including flavonoids, carotenoids, and ascorbic acid (vitamin C). By providing these essential nutrients, the researcher witnessed a significant increase in gastric tissue levels of protective compounds including glutathione, superoxide dismutase, and catalase activities. They concluded that a diet rich in fresh parsley leaf accelerates the healing process of duodenal or gastric ulcers (Akinci 2017). Making parsley leaf a regular addition to your diet may actually prevent the gastric injury that occurs as a consequence of a stress-filled lifestyle by protecting the mucus-producing layer of the gastrointestinal tract (Nielsen 1999, Teuscher 2005).

Parsley leaf is also used in traditional herbal medicine to treat intestinal disorders. This is especially true in spasm of the intestines. A recent laboratory study examined the effect of aqueous (water) and ethanolic (alcohol) extracts of parsley on spontaneous and acetylcholine-induced contractions on isolated rat intestinal tissue. Results showed that both water and ethanol extracts of parsley decreased spontaneous contractions of the intestinal tissues. Although both extracts were effective, the intestinal spasm reduction was greater with the ethanol extract than with the aqueous one (Brankovic 2010).

Parsley is also well known to help eliminate the smell of onion or garlic on the breath. James Duke (1997) writes about a friend who attended a high-class Persian dinner in the Washington D.C. area. At the center of the table, four large bowls were filled with the fresh leaves of coriander, parsley, spearmint, and tarragon. The guests rolled these leaves in pita bread, eating it to cleanse their palate between courses and to freshen their breath. Interestingly, these four herbs have been used as breath fresheners for centuries. Taking a hint from herbal medicine history, some manufacturers of garlic supplements add parsley to their products to minimize the smell of garlic on the breath. It is thought that chlorophyll found in parsley leaf may be responsible for its breath deodorant action (Duke 1997, Mésségué 1975).

Parsley seeds also possess substantial carminative and stomachic properties (Van Hellemont 1986). An infusion of the crushed seed expels intestinal gas, reduces flatulence, and soothes stomach and intestinal irritation and inflammation.

Parsley, Its Aquaretic Activity, and Simple Blood Pressure

In herbal medicine, an *aquaretic* herb is an herb that increases the excretion of water without causing the elimination of electrolytes. Many drugs used to increase the excretion of water also lead to the loss of important electrolytes such as sodium, chlorides, and potassium. These drugs may lead to serious negative health implications. For example, the loss of potassium may cause a dangerous, irregular heartbeat. Two herbs that have been most studied in the context of their aquaretic activity are asparagus (*Asparagus officinalis*) root and parsley leaf. In clinical trials, a combination of these two herbs caused significant weight loss in overweight patients who were also suffering from hypertension. More importantly, the water loss was achieved without leading to the loss of electrolytes (Bone 2013, Brankovic 2008).

Parsley and Anemia

Parsley leaf is known as a rich source of chlorophyll (Valnet 1977). In herbal medicine, plants that are rich in chlorophyll are used in as anti-anemic agents. This is based on the fact that chlorophyll has a structure that is very similar to hemoglobin, the oxygen-carrying portion of red blood cells. Chlorophyll provides the building blocks essential for our body to produce the hemoglobin we need.

Additionally, parsley leaf is also a rich source of iron; this mineral is essential for healthy red blood cell production. Since both chlorophyll and iron are needed by the body to build healthy blood, parsley leaf is an excellent addition to the diet. Greens, including parsley leaves, are regularly given to anemic people. Over a period of a few weeks, these individuals generally experience a healthy elevation of blood hemoglobin and total red blood cell levels (Valnet 1977) (Kirschmann 1996).

Parsley and Allergies

Parsley leaves are very rich in antihistaminic compounds called bioflav-onoids, including apigenin, luteolin, quercetin, and kampferol. Bioflavonoids are known to stabilize mast cells, the cells responsible for allergic reactions located throughout the mucous membranes of the respiratory, digestive, and urinary system as well as in the skin. When mast cells become hypersensitized, they become trigger happy. At the slightest provocation, like a grain of pollen, they release histamines, leukotrienes, and other substances that produce inflammation of the sinuses, lungs, digestive system, and skin. Eating parsley leaves on a regular basis provides your body with substantial amounts of bioflavonoids. These bioflavonoids stabilize mast cells and reduce allergies, asthma, itching of the skin and scalp, eczema, and other allergic manifestations (Duke 1985, Menzies-Trull 2003).

You know what that means, right? More parsley-laden tabbouleh, please.

Parsley Leaves, Coriander Leaves, and Heavy Metal Detoxification

Starting in the early 1990s, the use of cilantro (*Coriandrum sativum*) leaf has been advocated as a strategy to eliminate heavy metal accumulations, particularly those of mercury, from the human body. Many health advocates maintain that parsley leaf can be used for the same purpose as cilantro leaf.

The rationale behind the use of cilantro leaf for heavy metal chelation is that the constituents found in the leaf are thought to attach to heavy metals and promote their excretion out of the body. Much has been written about this controversial therapy. Proponents are staunchly adamant that ingestion of cilantro leaf results in a lessening of heavy metal load while opponents of the therapy argue that there is no scientific basis for the claims made by those advocating its use. In 1995 and 1996, Dr. Omura, MD, published two papers where he introduced the use of a bidigital O-ring test claimed to measure heavy metal levels in the body. He also proposed a protocol to remove heavy metals from the human body. In his clinical practice, Dr. Omura observed mercury blood levels rise after his patients had mercury dental amalgams removed. He had also noted that individuals who ate Vietnamese soup made with cilantro leaf experienced increasing excretion of mercury, lead, and aluminum. From these two observations, he started to treat patients exhibiting high heavy metal loads with 100 mg cilantro leaf tablets four times a day. He observed that levels of heavy metals dropped substantially (Omura 1995, Omura 1996). In the United States, Dr. Deitrich Klinghartd, MD., became a proponent of Dr. Omura's method and began teaching health professionals about his own specific protocol for heavy metals removal, including the use of cilantro extract.

Furthermore, Dr. Omura observed that eating cilantro leaf may reduce the absorption of heavy metals when it occurs at the same time as the heavy metal exposure. There is increasing evidence in animal studies that cilantro leaf used either prior to or at the same time as heavy metal or toxin exposure may protect the liver and other tissues from these exposures. In an animal study where mice were fed lead and cilantro leaves together, the study showed that ingestion of cilantro leaf reduced the negative effects of lead on liver enzymes, testosterone levels, and sperm density as well as the concentration of lead in the mice's gonads (Sharma 2010). In another animal study, mice were exposed to lead in their drinking water. The study concluded that cilantro leaf seemed to contain some type of unidentified chelating agent that binds and stimulates the excretion of lead. Cilantro leaf was shown to suppress lead deposition in the mice's bones and kidneys (Aga 2001). Another animal study showed that feeding cilantro leaf extract to rats prior to exposing them to liver toxins offered significant liver protection (Sreelatha 2009).

These studies imply that eating cilantro leaf with foods that contain elevated amounts of heavy metals or toxins may prevent their absorption in our body. I believe the same can be said for parsley leaf. For example, eating cilantro and/or parsley leaves with tuna or other fish that may contain significant amounts of heavy metals, may protect you from the heavy metals found in these foods. Given that higher levels of heavy metals are increasingly found in many types of foods, it is an excellent idea to incorporate the regular use of cilantro leaf and/or parsley leaf into our everyday diet. Purchase organic cilantro and/or parsley leaf for this purpose. Growing these two herbs in your garden and using them regularly in cooking is an excellent idea.

Parsley, Skin, Hair Health, and Insect Bites

Parsley leaf can be applied externally against fleeting pain, bruises, and contusions (injuries accompanied with blood vessel damages). The application of parsley leaf juice on the scalp has been shown to slow and stop the loss of hair. It is an excellent emergency remedy against insect bites (Mésségué 1975).

How to use Parsley as an Herbal Medicine

Internally:

Parsley Leaf: Pour boiling water over 1 gram (about 2/3 of a teaspoon) of the cut-and-sifted dried or fresh leaves. If using fresh, double the amount of parsley. Steep for 10 minutes in a covered cup, then strain. Take 30 drops of the liquid herbal extract in warm water 2 or 3 times a day at meal times. Add approximately 1 teaspoon to one tablespoon of the fresh leaves, minced, to your meal, sprinkled on your meal, or in your salad (Bartram 1998).

Juice from the fresh leaf can be made using a juicer. Use 5 drops of the fresh leaf juice directly in the ear to reduce the pain of an earache (Bartram 1998).

Parsley Seed: Fruits (although called commonly seeds) such as fennel, anise, caraway, dill, juniper, and parsley fruits contain volatile oils. To release these oils, these seeds need to be crushed or bruised before hot water is added (Schilcher 1997). To make the tea, steep one gram (about 2/3 of a teaspoon) of crushed parsley seeds in a cup of hot water for 5 to 10 minutes and filter. Take 2 or 3 cups per day. To use powdered parsley seed: take 1/2 teaspoon per dosage mixed well in water or juice, from 2 to 5 times a day. When making the tea of the seeds, do not boil (Van Hellemont 1986).

Parsley Root: Pour boiling water over 2 grams (about 1 heaping teaspoon) of finely cut dried or fresh root. Steep for 10 to 15 minutes in a covered cup. Strain. As a mild diuretic, drink 2 to 3 cups a day. In most instances, when making a tea from diverse medicinal roots, the usual recommendation is to boil them, However, when making the tea from parsley roots, it is recommended to not boil them but simply steep them (Van Hellemont 1986).

Externally:

Parsley leaf as a poultice: Often the bruised leaves are applied to swollen glands and swollen breasts to dry up milk. Hot fomentations wrung out of the tea will relieve insect bites and stings (Hutchens 1973).

Safety

The Botanical Safety Handbook classifies parsley leaf and root as a Class 1 herb, an herb that can be safely consumed when used appropriately (Gardner 2013). However, large doses of parsley should be avoided during pregnancy because parsley tends to stimulate the uterus (Mitchell 2003). Parsley seed and parsley essential oil in any amounts should **not** be used during pregnancy, since they are high in the constituent apiole making it unsafe during this period of time (Gardner 2013).

Contraindications

Pregnant women should eat only culinary or cooking amounts of parsley (Kirschmann 1996).

Side Effects

Allergic reactions of skin/mucosae (rarely) and phototoxicity may occur in some individuals. In one canning factory, the majority of the female workers handling and preparing parsley developed vesicular inflammation and purple discoloration of the skin and hands, followed by puberulent folliculitis and carbuncles. Oil of parsley used in perfumery has been known to cause dermatitis (Duke 1985, Teuscher 2005).

Parsley going to seed. *Stephanie Purello*

Drug Interactions

The Botanical Safety Handbook has classified parsley herb and root as a Class A herb, an herb for which no clinically relevant interactions are expected (Gardner 2013).

Kitchen tips

Do not buy powdered parsley seeds as they will lose their aroma and essential oils very quickly. Buy whole seeds and crush or powder them just before use. By following these recommendations, you'll access the full medicinal qualities of the seeds when you need them.

Whole dried seeds will keep for years when they are stored in hermetically-sealed glass or metal containers in an area low in moisture and free of light (Witchl 2004).

References

Aga, M., Iwaki, K., Ueda, Y., Ushio, S., Masaki N., Fukuda, S., Kimoto, T., Ikeda, M. and M. Kurimoto. 2001. Preventive effect of *Coriandrum sativum* (Chinese parsley) on localized lead deposition in ICR mice. *J Ethnopharmacol.* 77: 203-208.

Akinci, A., Esrefoglu, M., Taslidere, E., and B. Ates. 2017. *Petroselinum crispum* is effective in reducing stress-induced gastric oxidative damage. *Balkan M J* 34(1): 53-59.

Bartram, T. (1998) *Bartram's Encyclopedia of Herbal Medicine*. London, England: Constable and Robinson Ltd.

Bone. K. and S. Mills. (2013). *Principles and Practice of Phytotherapy*. 2nd ed. London, England: Churchill Livingstone.

Brankovic, S., Djosev, S., Kitic, D., et al. 2008. Hypotensive and negative chronotropic and inotropic effects of the aqueous and ethanol extract from parsley leaves. *J Clin Lipidol* 2(5) (Suppl 1): S191. S. 408.

Brankovic, S., Kitic, D., Radenkovic, M., Ivetic, V., Veljkovic, S., and M. Nesic. 2010. Relaxant activity of aqueous and ethanol extracts of parsley (*Petroselinum crispum* (Mill) Nym. ex. A. W Hill, Apiaceae) on isolated ileum of rat. Med Pregl. 63(7-8): 475-478.

Duke, J. 1985. *Handbook of Medicinal Herbs*, CRC Press.

Duke, J. 1997. *The Green Pharmacy*. St. Martin's Press.

Ellingwood, F. 1983 (First published in 1919). *American Materia Medica, Therapeutics and Pharmacognosy*. Eclectic Medical Publications.

Encyclopedia Britannica.com. 2020. https://www.britannica.com/sports/ Nemean-Games. Accessed on 8/9/20.

Felter, H. 1983. *The Eclectic Materia Medica, Pharmacology and Therapeutics*. Eclectic Medical Publications. (1922)

Fournier, P. 1948. *Le livre des plantes médicinales et vénéneuses de France*. Lechevalier, Paris, France.

Gardner, Z. and M. McGuffin. eds. 2013. *Botanical Safety Handbook*, 2 ed. Boca Raton, FL: CRC Press.

Grieve, M. 1971. *A Modern Herbal*. Dover Publications, Inc. (reprint of 1931 ed.).

Holmes, P. 1989. *The Energetic of Western Herbs*. Artemis Press.

Hutchens, A. 1973. *Indian Herbalogy of North America*. Merco.

Kirshmann, G.J. and Kirshmann J.D. 1996. *Nutrition Almanac*, 4 ed. McGraw-Hill.

Leclerc, H. 1929. *Les épices*. Paris, France: Masson.

Leclerc, H. 1976. *Précis de phytothérapie*. Paris, France: Masson.

Leung, A. and S. Foster. 1996. *Encyclopedia of Common Natural Ingredients used in Food, Drugs and Cosmetics*. 2 ed. John Wiley & Sons, Inc.

McGuffin, M., Kartesz, J.F., Leung, A.Y. and Tucker, A.O. 2000. *Herbs of Commerce*, 2 ed. American Herbal Products Association.

Menzies-Trull, C. 2003. *Herbal Medicine, Keys to Physiomedicalism including Pharmacopoeia*. Newcastle, England: Faculty of Physiomedical Herbal Medicine.

Mésségué, M. 1975. Mon herbier de santé. Paris, France: Laffont.

Mitchell, W. 2003. *Plant Medicine in Practice*. Elsevier Science.

Nickell, JM. 1976. *J.M. Nickell's Botanical Ready Reference*. CSA Press.

Nielsen, SE., Young, JF., Daneshvar, B.,. Lauridsen, ST., Knuthsen, P., Sandstro, B., and Dragsted, O. 1999. Effect of parsley (*Petroselinum crispum*) intake on urinary apigenin excretion blood antioxidant enzymes and biomarkers for oxidative stress in human. *Br. J. Nutr.* 81(6): 447-455.

Nissim, R. 1986. *Natural Healing in Gynecology*. Pandora Press.

Omura, Y, and Beckman, S.I. 1995. Role of mercury (Hg) in resistant infections and effective treatment of *Chlamydia trachomatis and Herpes* family viral infection (and potential treatment for cancer) by removing localized Hg deposits with Chinese parsley and delivering effective antibiotics using various drug uptake enhancement methods. *Acupunct Elecrother Res.* 50: 195-229.

Omura, Y., Shimotsuura, Y., Fukuoka, A., Fukuoka, H. and Nomoro, T. 1996. Significant mercury deposits in internal organs following the removal of dental amalgam, and development of pre-cancer on the gingiva and the sides of the tongue and their represented organs as a result of inadvertent exposure to strong curing light and effective treatment. *Acupunct Electrother Res.* 21: 133-160.

Rodriguez, D. 2020. "Celery: the aphrodisiac plant of Greek and Romans." http://www.dulcerodrigues.info/plantas/uk/aipo_uk.html. Accessed on 8/9/20.

Schilcher, H. 1997. *Phytotherapy in Paediatrics*. Stuttgart, Germany: Medpharm Scientific Publishers.

Sharma, V., Kansai, L. and A Sharma. 2010. Prophylactic efficacy of *Coriandrum sativum* (coriander) on testis of lead-exposed mice. *Biol Trace Elem Res.* 136: 337-354.

Sreelatha, S., Padma, P.R. and M. Umadevi. 2009. Protective effects of Coriandrum sativum extracts on carbon tetrachloride-induced hepatotoxicity in rats. *Food Chem Toxicol.* 47: 702-708.

Stansbury, J. 2018. *Herbal Formularies for Health Professionals Vol. 1. Digestion and Elimination*. Chelsea Green Publishing.

Teuscher, E., Anton, R. and A. Lobstein. 2005. *Plantes Aromatiques*. Paris,

France: Editions Tec et Doc.

Trickey, R. 1998. *Women, Hormones & Menstrual Cycle*. St. Leonards, Australia: Allen & Unwin.

Uphof, J.C. 1968. Dictionary of Economic Plants. Stechert-Harner Service Agency, Inc.

Valnet, J. 1977. *Traitement des maladies par les légumes, les fruits, et les céréales*. Paris, France: Maloine.

Van Hellemont, J. 1986. *Compendium de Phytothérapie*. Brussels, Belgium: Association Pharmaceutique Belge.

Western Institute for Food Safety and Security. 2016. *Parsley*. Davis, CA: https://www.wifss.ucdavis.edu/wp-content/uploads/2016/10/Parsley_PDF. pdf. Accessed 7/18/2020.

Wichtl, M. (Ed.) 2004. *Herbal Drugs and Phytopharmaceuticals*. 3 ed. CRC Press.

Wren, RB. 1988. *Potter's New Cyclopaedia of Botanical Drugs and Preparations*. Revised by E. Williamson. Essex, England: The C.W. Daniel Company Limited.

Yarnell, E., Abascal, K. and CG Hooper. (2003). *Clinical Botanical Medicine*. Mary Ann Liebert, Inc.

Daniel Gagnon, Medical Herbalist, MS, RH (AHG) is a French-Canadian originally from Ontario who relocated to Santa Fe, NM in 1979. He has been a practicing Medical Herbalist since 1976. Daniel is the author of *The Practical Guide to Herbal Medicines*, a book designed to provide herbal health care options. He is also the co-author of *Breathe Free*, a book on healing the respiratory system. He regularly teaches herbal therapeutics both nationally and internationally. Daniel is the owner of Herbs, Etc., an herbal medicine retail store and manufacturing facility. www.herbsetc.com. Daniel can be reached at botandan@aol.com.

Parsley Leaf Scan II. *Stephanie Parello*

Health Inducing Parsley

Carol Little, R.H

Parsley is so much more than a garnish! Who doesn't remember that toasted grilled cheese from the diner with that sprig of green parsley for decoration? In North America, this nutrient-dense herb has for years played the part of greenery on a plate to spruce up many a restaurant meal. There's SO much more to parsley.

Parsley (*Petroselinum crispum*) is a species of Petroselinum, a member of the family of Apiaceae plants. Other plants in this family include anise, carrots, celery, cumin, and dill. Both types, the curly parsley and the flat leaf or Italian parsley, are common in gardens, garden centres, farmers markets, and grocery stores.

Native to Mediterranean countries, parsley is an integral part of many cuisines in the region. These cultures have grown and used parsley extensively for centuries in their meals and in traditional folk medicine as diuretics, anti-inflammatory aids, digestives, and detoxification remedies. Parsley contains several important nutrients, such as vitamins A, C, and K. It's also an excellent source of folic acid plus the minerals calcium, iron, magnesium and potassium. In fact, 2 tablespoons (8 grams) of parsley herb provide:

- **Calories**: 2
- **Vitamin A**: 12% of the Reference Daily Intake (RDI)
- **Vitamin C**: 16% of the RDI
- **Vitamin K**: 154% of the RDI

Vitamin A is probably most famous as a support for our eyes but it is also a good support to our immune system. It's renowned for skin health too and is often a part of skin condition treatments. **Vitamin C** is vital to our immune system function, supportive of cardiovascular health and a powerful antioxidant, which can protect our cells from damage caused by the infamous 'free radicals' (unstable molecules). **Vitamin K** is essential for optimum blood clotting, which can prevent excessive bleeding. This important nutrient also supports heart and bone health.

Parsley's essential oil contains myristicin, limonene, eugenol, and alpha-thujene. According to an article in the *Journal of the Science of Food and Agriculture*, these compounds can benefit the body's immune system, neutralizing oxidative stress and fighting off carcinogens. In fact, studies show that essential oils in parsley can actually slow tumour growth in cancer cases. *Eugenol*, in particular, has strong anti-inflammatory properties and is thought to help to alleviate the swelling and pain caused by arthritic conditions and other inflammatory issues.

Parsley Benefits

More formal studies are needed but a growing body of evidence suggests that parsley may offer multiple benefits, which, according to herbologist Mark Pedersen, may help with the following imbalances:

- Acid reflux
- Anemia
- Arthritis
- Atherosclerosis
- Bad breath
- Bladder infection
- Bloating/edema
- Blood sugar
- Cancer (research indicates specific types of cancer helped)
- Constipation
- Digestive problems, including irritable bowel syndrome
- Gas
- Inflammation
- Kidney stones
- Oxidative stress/free radical damage
- Poor immunity
- Skin problems

After reading that lengthy list above, we can see how finding more ways to include parsley in our diets is a great idea.

Parsley tea/juice has been a traditional remedy for soothing the digestive system and decreasing tummy aches, supporting the kidneys and liver in detoxification processes. Parsley tea can help to soothe the throat. Asthmatic patients may benefit from this because parsley is a slight expectorant that helps to ease coughs, release mucus, and improve breathing. In fact, it can act as a sort of natural anti-histamine to relieve allergies, hay fever, and other respiratory issues.

Herbalists may suggest a juice or a tea made from the leaves or roots or simply the practice of including MORE parsley in your meals. Everything is a habit! Eat more parsley! Read on for some of my all-time favourite ways to boost enjoyment of this super nutritious herbal ally.

Parsley Digestive Tea

This fragrant tea can settle digestion nicely. Ginger root and parsley herb together can help to soothe nausea in cases of stomach flu. Fennel seeds and parsley herb together can help increase movement in cases of stagnant digestion. This combination can also help to alleviate flatulence and bloating. Crush the seeds slightly first for a stronger, more fragrant tea.

2 to 4 tablespoons of fresh parsley leaves
2 cups good quality water
1 tablespoon grated ginger root, optional
1 tablespoon fennel seed, optional

Place the parsley, ginger, and fennel in a glass jar or teapot. Add boiling water. Place the lid on the jar or pot. Allow to steep for 10 minutes (or to your preference).

Harvest parsley stems at the base of the plant, cutting them from the outermost ring of stems (not from the middle of the plant) and put them in a jar of water. They will last on the kitchen counter for a week or two.
Susan Belsinger

From the Herbalist's Point of View

Herbalists tend to think of parsley with specific ideas in mind, as a medicinal herb. I find that parsley as a **carminative** is very helpful to improve poor digestion, bloating, gas, and constipation. We use carminatives to help people with a poor appetite, and those who need to "get the plumbing humming". Even just a few sprigs of parsley eaten prior to consuming a meal can help to improve assimilation.

Parsley is typically thought of as a **diuretic** remedy and is well known for positive effects on the urinary system, especially in cases of cystitis (also known as urinary tract infection or UTI), edema, painful urination, and kidney stones. Parsley roots are stronger than leaves and are sometimes made into a strong decoction in these cases.

Parsley can be used to stimulate uterine contractions to help to bring on a delayed menses or in specific cases of amenorrhea (lack of menstruation). I have used parsley as an **emmenagogue** in my herb practice to help in both these cases, with good results. Note: Although parsley is only a mild uterine stimulant, it's best to **avoid** large doses during pregnancy. If pregnant, consuming parsley as a food is not an issue.

You may notice that in all three areas, above, there is a sense of movement. I noticed this years ago and began to use parsley in other areas as well, when the need for "movement" exists in the body. Parsley can stimulate areas of the body where stagnation and other types of inflammation exist. Similar to dandelion leaf, parsley can help to dispel fluids from the body without depleting potassium.

Parsley contains carotenoid antioxidants and vitamins, both of which have been shown to benefit heart health. It seems that these components plus the specific essential oils in parsley combine to support overall heart health and healthy arteries as well. Parsley is also known to be beneficial to blood circulation; as a type of vasodilator, it has been noted to help with the widening of blood vessels and to open up the blood passageways throughout the body. Carotenoid-rich diets have been shown to reduce heart disease risk factors like chronic inflammation, elevated blood pressure, and high LDL (bad) cholesterol levels.

I don't know if there is a therapeutic dose, as we call it in herbalism, where a specific amount of an herb is needed before a change is noted. I do know that it's a lot more than a parsley sprig as a garnish. Enjoy often!

Here are some easy ways to add parsley to your daily meals:

Fresh parsley adds pizazz to pizza. *Susan Belsinger*

- Add to homemade bread, rolls or bagels
- Use on homemade pizza, alone or with other greens
- Use in quiches, scrambles, or frittatas
- Make a pesto with parsley as the star or a green blend of basil plus parsley or dandelion plus parsley
- Include in vinaigrettes or marinades
- Make homemade juice combinations or add to morning smoothies to create nutrient-dense drinks
- Add flavour to sauces, soups, and stews
- Use as a rub to add flavour to poultry, meat, and fish dishes
- Chop to make a salad, or add to salads

To increase your parsley consumption, here are some of my own recipes and selections from friends around the world, starting with a delicious hummus. Aryn Mahood, my dear friend from Sweet Song Herbals, writes: "Oh I love parsley!! I started using it as a digestive aid. One of my best friends can't eat hummus because it gives her awful gas. So I started making it with huge amounts of parsley... and voila! No gas! So my hummus is green!"

Sweet Song Green Hummus

I like it good and garlicky, but you can use less. A dash or two of cayenne pepper adds a warm finish to this hummus.

Makes 8 servings

3 to 8 cloves garlic

2 15-ounce cans chickpeas, drained
2 lemons, juiced
2 to 4 teaspoons olive oil
1 teaspoon sesame oil
1 teaspoon cumin
Dash sea salt
Dash cayenne pepper powder
1 large bunch fresh parsley, chopped

Add garlic to your food processor and mince. Add the chick peas, sesame oil, and lemon juice. Drizzle in olive oil to desired consistency. Add salt, cumin and cayenne. Add parsley. Continue processing. Serve with veggies or slathered on a pita, fresh bread, or your favourite crackers.

Diana De Luca, author, herbalist, teacher, and mentor, shared these parsley ideas with me recently. I confess to being addicted to her Quick Parsley Salad below. I hope you'll try it! Diana is definitely one of my all-time favourite herbalists and one of the legendary "Garlic Queens". I was always in the front row of any class she taught at the annual Women's Herbal Conference. Using food as medicine, Diana makes a yummy parsley salad to keep away and help treat urinary tract infections as well as nourish our bodies and spirits.

Quick Parsley Salad

Diana De Luca describes this as "Italian parsley drizzled with a little olive oil, a pinch of sea salt, lemon juice and a thin drizzle of maple syrup smashed up with your hands and allowed to sit a few minutes".

Makes 2 servings

1 bunch of flat leaf parsley, chopped
2 tablespoons olive oil
1 pinch sea salt
2 tablespoons maple syrup
Juice of 1 lemon
Lemon zest, optional
Garlic, minced, optional

Place all ingredients in a large bowl. Smash all together with your hands. Wash your hands and enjoy!

Diana's Gremolata

Traditionally, gremolata would be used as an additional level of flavour to meat dishes like grilled lamb or beef. I've served it with heavy meat dishes, but on the side, and it's a crowd-pleaser! I often make a big batch and freeze extra in small jars or even in ice cube trays. Optional additions: 1 teaspoon rosemary, fresh, minced; 1 teaspoon dried or fresh oregano, minced; handful spearmint fresh leaves, finely chopped; or go wild with finely minced, freshly picked fir needles.

Makes 2 to 4 servings

1 to 2 cloves garlic, minced
2 teaspoons lemon zest
3 tablespoons olive oil
Pinch sea salt
Pinch cayenne pepper, optional
1 cup fresh Italian parsley, chopped

Place the garlic, lemon zest, olive oil, salt, and cayenne, if using, in a bowl with the chopped parsley.

Mix well with a wooden spoon. Taste. Adjust seasonings.

Store in glass jars in the fridge for 3 to 4 days. It should keep for up to 2 weeks if there is a little film of olive oil over the top, covering the ingredients. It will also freeze well. Label and it's ready to enjoy all year round.

Note: To make a larger batch, just double or triple the ingredients and use a food processor to whip up in a flash. Place the parsley, lemon zest and garlic in the food processor. Give it a whirl. Add the olive oil and seasonings next and pulse a few times. It's ready to slather and enjoy with friends or family. I have come to see this 'processed' gremolata as a kind of versatile herby sauce which can be swirled into warm pasta or tossed with potatoes or beans. It's magical drizzled over roasted veggies or a simple avocado toast.

Parsley Potatoes

I've made these for years and often combine with lemon balm for additional flavour. These are classic taters and a very elegant presentation. The amount of parsley used here can vary from 2 to 10 tablespoons, depending upon the desired result. Experiment to see what suits you.

2 pounds new potatoes
3 to 4 tablespoons butter or good quality olive oil
Sea salt and freshly ground pepper
Fresh parsley leaves, finely chopped

Add the potatoes to a medium saucepan and cover with cold water by 2 inches. Bring to a boil and add about 1 teaspoon sea salt. Reduce to a simmer and cook until potatoes are fork tender, about 15 to 20 minutes. Drain the water from the pot.

Stir butter into the potatoes. Add the chopped parsley, then season with a little freshly ground pepper and sea salt. Mix well. Serve hot.

Parsley Compound Butter

Compound butters can be as simple or complex as you want. I love to add finely minced local garlic, snippets of rosemary, thyme, sage, lemon balm, savoury, or whatever beckons from my garden. I've made simple parsley butter with a little onion and/or garlic powder too, with good success. The sky's the limit. Do you like bleu cheese? This addition can result in a very elegant butter to serve atop a juicy BBQ steak.

If you plan to use all of your compound butter immediately, you can use fresh parsley and herbs right from your garden. If your plan is to make a parsley butter that will last more than 3 to 4 days, you can use the dried herb. I prefer to use fresh herbs and make some to use today or tomorrow and freeze the remainder. I prefer unsalted, freshly churned butter and add a little good quality sea salt to control the amount of salt, but you can also use salted butter. Just omit any additional salt. The amount or combination of herbs can vary depending upon your own taste and goal for the finished product.

2 sticks unsalted butter (approximately 1 cup), softened
1 teaspoon sea salt
4 to 5 tablespoons fresh parsley, finely chopped
1 to 3 cloves garlic, finely chopped, optional

Cream the butter, salt, parsley, and garlic together in a bowl. Cover and store in the refrigerator for 3 hours before using. The butter will keep for several days, if it lasts that long.

Alternatively, after creaming the ingredients together, turn out onto a small sheet of parchment paper or plastic wrap and roll into a tight cylinder. Refrigerate or freeze for later use. This method allows for an elegant presentation, with the slice of the cylinder creating a buttery disc, placed atop a steak or vegetable dish. The cylinder roll method does require an additional step but is a wonderful idea, and worth the time if you are looking for this sort of presentation.

Persillesovs or Parsley Gravy

Here's a classic recipe courtesy of my Swedish friend Mona Petersen. She and her Danish husband Borge are proprietors of Westwood Gardens, just east of Peterborough, Ontario. This is a traditional Danish recipe and a family favourite. It can be served over potatoes or in a dish called "Stekt flask med persiljesas", a classic crispy pork dish with boiled potatoes. Mona says that this delicious parsley gravy goes especially well with potatoes and any pork dish.

1/4 cup (20 grams) butter
1/3 cup (25 grams) all-purpose flour
1.5 cups (350 ml) milk or vegetable broth
1/2 teaspoon salt
1/4 teaspoon white pepper
2 tablespoons parsley, finely chopped

Melt the butter in a saucepan on medium heat. Slowly add the flour, stirring constantly with a fork or a whisk. Gradually add the milk or broth and increase heat to medium-high, stirring continually. The gravy will thicken in about 10 minutes. Add the salt and white pepper and mix well. Add the parsley and combine well. Serve hot.

Traditional Lebanese Tabbouleh

A discussion of parsley in our meals wouldn't be complete without the famous Middle Eastern salad, Tabbouleh. My sister-in-law is married to a very talented Lebanese chef and was kind enough to share this recipe. As with any centuries old recipe, there will be many variations, but this one from my extended family is delicious. Yvonne prefers whole wheat bulgur, but white will do just as well. Note: The North African or Middle Eastern Seven Spices is a blend that can be found at specialty shops or you can make your own using black pepper, cinnamon, cloves, coriander, cumin, ginger, and nutmeg.

Serves 4

1 bunch curly parsley, well washed, stems removed and very finely chopped
3/4 of English cucumber, peeled, seeded and finely chopped
2 large, very firm tomatoes, finely chopped
2 to 3 green onions finely chopped
Juice of half a lemon
1/4 cup fine (#1) bulgur wheat
1/8 cup olive oil
Sea salt and pepper
1/2 teaspoon Seven Spice Blend, optional

Place the bulgur into a flat bowl, like a soup bowl, adding just enough room temperature water to cover.

Let sit while preparing the other ingredients.

Place chopped parsley, cucumber, tomatoes, and green onions into a large bowl and mix together. Add lemon juice, olive oil, seasonings, and the bulgur, which should now be soft and damp. If any water is still visible in the bulgur bowl, gently scoop bulgur out by hand and squeeze out water over the sink before adding to salad. Discard any water in bowl when bulgur has been removed.

Mix salad well in bowl, serve, and enjoy. These ingredients can easily be doubled. This salad is unusual as it keeps well in the fridge for up to 6 days.

Parsley Wine

I am a big fan of Hildegard of Bingen, who was born in Germany in 1098. St. Hildegard (canonized in 2012) was a remarkable woman: a Benedictine abbess, accomplished poet, avid composer, visionary, and revered herbalist. I love her music and have greatest respect for her herbal teachings. According to her teachings, parsley wine is a remedy against cardiac insufficiency, heart failure, poor circulation, weakness, stress-based nervous heart pain, valve defects, and for detoxification after viral infections. "Whoever suffers from pain in the heart, spleen or side, drink this wine often (daily) and it will heal him."

Parsley wine (also known as parsley-honey wine) has repeatedly proven to be an effective remedy for rheumatic heart pain or weakness of the heart during flu season. For any weakness of the heart, especially in old age, Hildegard suggested parsley wine first before any medicine is given, as it usually takes care of symptoms without using any chemicals. Parsley wine is also thought to be very helpful for rehabilitation after a heart attack to remove residual pain. The essential oils in parsley are thought to have a cramp-easing influence on the heart and circulatory system.

Boiling honey and wine together is said to produce a heart and circulation strengthening glucoside. This beverage makes a tasty aperitif, reputed to improve and strengthen health and well-being. I have shared the original recipe but I have seen variations made with white wine as well. I prefer white wine personally but for this heart tonic, I always make it with organic, heart-healthy red wine.

8 to 10 sprigs fresh parsley
1 quart organic red wine
2 tablespoons wine vinegar, white or red
1 cup raw honey

Boil parsley, wine, and wine vinegar for 5 to 10 minutes. Add honey and boil again 5 more minutes.

Skim off the foam, then pour through a sieve into a funnel and then back into the wine bottle. Label. Store in cool dark cupboard.

How to Use: Take 1 shot glass 3 times a day after meals. Keep away from children.

Parsley Herb Paste

If we are serious about upping the parsley quotient in our daily meals, there's a great way to preserve its goodness during the growing season for use in the cold months. I make herb pastes from many of my culinary and medicinal herbs. An easy herb paste is my go-to method for preserving the high nutrient content of parsley for use all year long. It's so easy.

1 bunch fresh parsley
Good quality olive oil

Place the washed parsley in a food processor. Drizzle in the olive oil. Pulse a few times. Use a spatula or wooden spoon to scrape the sides of the container to ensure all ingredients are incorporated. Add enough olive oil so that the parsley becomes a thick paste.

Spoon into a glass canning jar and top with a thin layer of oil. Alternatively, spoon into ice cube trays and freeze. Afterwards, store in airtight plastic bags, or freezer-worthy containers. In either case, it's always a good idea to date and label the container.

Parsley, so full of vitamins, minerals and antioxidants, is considered by many to be a superfood. There are so many great reasons to enjoy this herb. I hope I have made you think about your own possibilities. Parsley truly deserves to be liberated from its status as mere garnish, don't you think? Go Parsley!

References

Bingen, Hildegard. *Healthy Hildegard.* www.healthyhildegard.com/health-benefits-parsley-wine/. Accessed 01/09/20.

De Luca, Diana. Personal phone call. July 12, 2020.

----- *Botanica Erotica: Arousing Body, Mind, and Spirit.* Healing Arts Pres, 1998.

Little, Carol. "Delicious DIY 7 Spice Blend Recipes." *StudioBotanica.* www.studiobotanica.com/easy-diy-7-spices-blend/. Accessed 01/09/20.

Mahoud, Aryn. "Green Hummus." https://www.sweetsong.ca.

Pedersen, Mark. *Nutritional Herbology.* Wendell W. Whitman Co, 1987.131-133.

Peterson, Mona and Borge. Personal interview. June 28, 2020.

Tang, Esther Lai-Har, Jayakumar Rajarajeswaran and MS Kanthimathi. "Petroselinum crispum has antioxidant properties, protects against DNA damage and inhibits proliferation and migration of cancer cells." *Journal of the Science of Food and Agriculture.* onlinelibrary.wiley.com/doi/full/10.1002/jsfa.7078. Accessed 01/09/20.

Carol Little, R.H. is a traditional herbalist in Toronto, Canada, where she has a private practice working primarily with women. Her easy-to-digest weekly blog posts offer quick takeaway ideas to help readers feel their best (https://www.studiobotanica.com). Check out her active Facebook community at https://www.facebook.com/studiobotanica and follow her on Instagram https://www.instagram.com/studiobotanica.

Carol is a current professional and past board member of the Ontario Herbalists Association. She combines her love of travel and passion for all things green to write about both. Carol has written for *Vitality Magazine* and the monthly online *Natural Herbal Living Magazine*. She has been a regular contributor to the *Home Herbalist* magazine as well as the IHA annual Herb of the Year™ book. She is a proud participant in the recently published *FIRE CIDER101 Zesty Recipes for Health-Boosting Remedies* by Rosemary Gladstar and friends.

This photo was taken in the Heritage Herb Garden at the Ozark Folk Center, where there is a featured Herb of the Year bed every year. Parsley is great to use in plantings with vegetables and flowers too—it likes a humus-rich soil just like most veggies—and straw mulch. *Susan Belsinger*

Baby seedlings of parsley were started with a few seeds in each cell of a seed flat. These are ready to be transplanted. *Susan Belsinger*

Pondering Parsley

Jane Hawley Stevens

As I sit at my desk chewing a stalk of parsley, I consider what to love most about the welcoming and pleasant presence of this delightful herb. After all, its message is one of festivity, according to the Victorian lore revealing the hidden messages of flowers and herbs. Typically, I plant it near my front door yearly to bring in friends and festivity. This year I did not, but it remains nearby, for small socially distant gatherings.

Curly parsley (*Petroselinum crispum* var. *crispum*) makes a great border to flower beds, staying compact, dark green, and cheery all summer and into winter. Planted near the kitchen, I have easy access for salads or cooked foods. It takes about one-half cup of parsley a day to meet 54% of the recommended vitamin C and 554% of vitamin K! Munching on this pungent package of green goodness, I feel its nutrient-rich potency freshen my mouth and begin to release its storehouse of vitamins and minerals, making my day brighter already.

I wonder what the Greeks knew, who also planted parsley around their flower beds. After all, Homer writes about feeding chariot horses parsley to maintain their strength.

My summer mornings are often blessed with gathering herbs, vegetables, and fruits to blend together for a smoothie, of sorts. Many would not like my blends of red cabbage, blackberries, parsley, lemon balm, ladies' mantle, nettles or whatever speaks to me that day! I like to collect my vitamins right from the garden, when possible.

Parsley seeds are among the first packet I gather from my chilled seed box in the early spring. They are not long lived, so don't keep them past two years. They are slow to germinate, preferring spring's cooler temperatures and can be planted before the last frost. This trifecta finds me loving this crop one more time, initiating my favorite ritual of the year—germinating seeds. Sow parsley with early lettuce, cabbages, and perennials.

The Italian variety can bolt under intense heat, even though it is a biennial. This is another reason I prefer the curly parsley in Wisconsin—it lasts until it is covered by snow. A way to avoid losing your Italian parsley mid-summer is to cut off the flowering stalks as soon as they develop, fertilize with fish emulsion, and water well to keep the plant growing vegetatively.

Parsley is one of the few culinary herbs that grows in part shade and, because of its petite stature, does well in containers on porches and decks. Maude Grieve recommends sowing seeds again in August for greenhouses or cold frames. Plant at 6- to 8-inch intervals.

If someone asked a person who was not an herbalist if they thought parsley was loaded with nutrients, I bet they would instinctively say yes—providing they have had more tastes than that limp fragment found on restaurant plates. The potent flavors and deep, dark green are clues to its power. The constituents in parsley have been found to offer major health benefits, including heart and vascular health, urinary tract health, eye health, and the cancer protective flavone *apigenin*.

Anticancer

The flavone apigenin is particularly concentrated in parsley and other members of the Apiaceae family and has been the subject of considerable research. The National Cancer Institute includes parsley in the group of plants that have the highest anticancer properties, along with other Apiaceae, garlic, and soybeans. An added plus is these compounds are heat stable and do not degrade when cooking. The high concentration of vitamin C in parsley contributes to its anti-cancer benefits, by reducing oxidative stress, or lowering the free radicals, which damage cells.

Eye Health

Parsley is so high in vitamin A that it is listed as a great plant source for eye health. My sister-in-law, Liz Johnson, PhD, works for Tufts and has investigated the link between lutein and eye health. Her takeaway for optimal eye health to the family is, "Just eat dark green and yellow- or orange-colored vegetables and make sure these are part of your daily diet." Parsley is certainly in this rank! Liz continues, "Vitamin A is fat soluble and is stored in your fat cells; so if you do not eat it every day, it will be there for your body's optimal health. If your hands have a bit of yellow tinge on the palms, it means you are getting plenty of vitamin A."

Bone Density

Parsley is uncommonly rich in vitamin K. This particular vitamin plays a protective role in vascular health and bone density. Eating foods rich in vitamin K has been linked to reduced fractures and improved bone mineral density. In fact, a Nurse's Health Study found that those who get at least 110 micrograms (mcg) of vitamin K are 30% less likely to break a hip compared to those who eat fewer greens (*International Osteoporosis Foundation*). Bring on the parsley!

Healthy Urinary Function

The German Commission E, Germany's equivalent of our FDA, lists parsley as a bladder tonic and a diuretic, promoting liver and kidney functions. Because of that action, it is also helpful in the case of urinary disorders and can be useful for UTI's, with increased water intake. In Chinese medicine, parsley is said to harmonize the bladder, nourish the blood, and relieve fatigue, and is called a digestive restorative or liver yin tonic. In the Chinese tradition, parsley is said to help with blood deficiency, pale complexion, weak nails, fatigue, and anemia. According to herbalist Peter Holmes, parsley root can be briefly decocted (simmered for 10 minutes) or used in tincture form.

Parsley seed should not to be used in large quantities during pregnancy because it relaxes the uterus and tends to open up things and move them out. (This is the doctrine of signatures, observing the morphology or looks of a plant to find clues to their uses. Picture the leaves sprouting from the crown moving upward and outward.) Its cousin, the wild carrot, *Daucus carota*, has historically been used by women to stay free from pregnancy. My 100-year old neighbor told me about the woman who lived across the road, keeping herself childless with the help of Queen Anne's Lace, or wild carrot seed. In fact, in Chinese medicine there is a remedy which translates as "Worry-Free Formula to Protect Birth". This remedy is given after the sixth month of pregnancy to ensure the baby is positioned right and to ensure a smooth delivery.

Parsley is considered a digestive restorative, like fennel, asparagus root, and celery root. Even Gerard says, "It is delightful to the taste and agreeable to the stomache." This is why I grow a flat of parsley every year to include in meals any way I can think of. You can use the stems for an extra crunch, especially great in potato salads. Here's to growing and eating parsley!

Ways to Increase Parsley in Your Diet

🌿 Add to salad dressings.

🌿 Coarsely chop over salads, fish or chicken for a garnish that will be eaten!

🌿 Add to smoothies for a great fresh taste.

🌿 Add to pesto. I use 50% basil and 50% parsley and that is delicious!

🌿 Nibble on leaves or stalks as a breath freshener while weeding or strolling through the garden.

Jane's Classic Salad Dressing

1 cup extra virgin olive oil
1 cup Bragg's cider vinegar or balsamic vinegar
2 tablespoons honey
3 tablespoons chopped fresh parsley
3 tablespoons chopped aromatic herbs like basil, lemon basil, lemon balm, French tarragon, lemongrass, lemon verbena, dill, or fennel
Salt and pepper

Place all ingredients in a blender. Blend until particles are small enough to flow through the dressing. Store in a wine bottle or your favorite salad dressing bottle.

Add to salads as desired. Enjoy!

References

Chang, Hui, Lin Lei , Yun Zhou , Fayin Ye, and Guohua Zhao. "Dietary Flavonoids and the Risk of Colorectal Cancer: An Updated Meta-Analysis of Epidemiological Studies." *Nutrients*. 2018 Jul 23;10 (7):950. Accessed 10/13/20.

Craig, A. J. "Phytochemicals in Herbs Reduce Disease." *HerbClip American Botanical Council*. 9/9/98. http://cms.herbalgram.org/herbclip/140/review42094.html. Accessed 10/13/20.

Faustino, Jacqueline Ferreira, Alfredo Ribeiro-Silva, Rodrigo Faeda Dalto, Marcelo Martins de Souza, João Marcello Fortes Furtado, Gutemberg de Melo Rocha, Monica Alves, and Eduardo Melani Rocha. "Vitamin A and the eye: an old tale for modern times." *PubMed.gov*. pubmed.ncbi.nlm.nih.gov/26840172/. Accessed 8/18/20.

Grieve, Mrs. M. "Parsley." *A Modern Herbal. Botanical.com*. botanical.com/botanical/mgmh/p/parsle09.html. Accessed 10/13/20.

Holmes, Peter. *The Energetics of Western Herbs*. Snow Lotus Press, 1989.

Liz Johnson, PhD. Personal interview. 9/20/20.

"Vitamin K—new research shows that this 'forgotten' vitamin may be good for your bone health." *International Osteoporosis Foundation*. July 17, 2015. https://www.iofbonehealth.org/news/vitamin-k-may-be-good-for-your-bone-health. Accessed 7/18/20.

Jane Hawley Stevens is the 2020 Organic Farmer of the Year and founder of Four Elements Organic Herbals, in North Freedom, Wisconsin, established in 1987. Jane is a pioneer in organic farming and the natural products communities, and has been certified organic since 1990. Jane grows and harvests herbs on her 130-acre certified organic farm to create various wellness products, sold online and throughout the country. She just received a USDA Value Added Producers Grant to expand online marketing. Her passions are plant propagation, practicing gardening, and living by the moon cycles while educating through her writing and presentations.

Plant parsley with other herbs in a container near your kitchen. *Gert Coleman*

Bios for Illustrators and Photographers

Susan Belsinger—see bio on page 8.

Gert Coleman—see bio on page 65.

Peter Coleman grows trees, herbs, vegetables and at-risk plants in Middlefield, New York. A Master Gardener, Peter photographs woods, trees, streams, plants, and the world from social, political, and historical perspectives.

Karen England—see bio on page 116.

Deb Jolly is the Plant, Arbor, and Greenhouse Specialist at Ozark Folk Center State Park in Mountain View, Arkansas, where she specializes in plant propagation. She is a member of the Ozark Unit of The Herb Society of America. A self-proclaimed naturalist, Deb enjoys capturing all aspects of nature in photographs.

Pat Kenny has been a medical illustrator (retired from NIH); volunteer herb publicist giving photo-illustrated herb talks and demos neighborhood-to-nation; member of IHA since it was IHGMA; member of HSA since 1979; and supporter of the nation's largest public herb garden, the National Herb Garden in Washington, DC, which has stimulated her curiosity about the world of herbal plants. Pat serves as Vice President of IHA.

Alicia Mann is a classically trained artist and metalsmith at Heritage Metalworks, LTD, in Downington, Pennsylvania. A graduate of Maryland Institute College of Art, she integrates her interests in art and horticulture by growing flowers, herbs, vegetables, and fruit trees. Alicia's endearing and professional illustrations introduce the three sections of *Parsley*. ammann1212@gmail.com

Cooper T. Murray—see bio on page 156.

Theresa Mieseler—see bio on page 145.

Stephanie Parello—see bio on page 78.

Skye Suter—see bio on page 182.

Gail Wood Miller is a member of the Musconetcong Watercolor Group, and of the Garden State Watercolor Society. Drawing and painting have been hobbies since childhood. Her day job is health and education coach and consultant, focusing on women and children. A retired professor of English and English education, she also speaks and writes about individual learning styles. The parsley is painted in black gouche.

Cover Credits

Front Cover:

Background image: Flat and curly leafed parsley side by side.
Susan Belsinger

Back Cover:

Left: Flowering umbel. *Susan Belsinger*

Middle: Parsley for fun, flavor and festivies. *Susan Belsinger*

Right: Hamburg parsley root. *Deb Jolly*

Section Illustrations:

Alicia Mann's illustrations grace the section introductions
on pages xii, 74, and 184.

Celebrating 25 Years of Herb of the Year™!

How the Herb of the Year™ is Selected

Every year since 1995, the International Herb Association has chosen an Herb of the Year™ to highlight. The Horticultural Committee evaluates possible choices based on their being outstanding in at least two of the three major categories: medicinal, culinary, or decorative. Many other herb organizations support the herb of the year selection and we work together to educate the public about these herbs during the year.

Herbs of the Year™: Past, Present and Future

1995	Fennel	2011	Horseradish
1996	Monarda	2012	Rose
1997	Thyme	2013	Elderberry
1998	Mint	2014	Artemisia
1999	Lavender	2015	Savory
2000	Rosemary	2016	Capsicum
2001	Sage	2017	Cilantro & Coriander
2002	Echinacea	2018	Humulus
2003	Basil	2019	Agastache
2004	Garlic	2020	Rubus
2005	Oregano & Marjoram	2021	Parsley
2006	Scented Geraniums	2022	Viola
2007	Lemon Balm	2023	Ginger
2008	Calendula	2024	Yarrow
2009	Bay Laurel	2025	Chamomile
2010	Dill		

Books available on www.iherb.org

Join the IHA

Associate with other herb businesses and like-minded folks, network and have fun while you are doing it!

Membership Levels:

$50 Individual Professional
$50 Affiliate Professional
$50 Post Secondary Student

Log onto www.iherb.org to see what we are all about!

Membership includes:

Your business information listed on www.iherb.org
Membership directory
Herb of the Year™ publication
Quarterly newsletters
Online herbal support
Discounts on conference fees
Promotional support for IHA's Herb of the Year program and
National Herb Week
Support for National Herb Day
Assocation with a network of diverse herbal businesses

CPSIA information can be obtained
at www.ICGtesting.com
Printed in the USA
FSHW021714040421
80110FS